D0604206

ZEN

THE ART OF MODERN EASTERN COOKING

ZEN

THE ART OF MODERN EASTERN COOKING

DENG MING-DAO

INTRODUCTION BY EDWARD ESPE BROWN
FEATURING THE FOOD OF ARNOLD WONG
AND WITH CONTRIBUTIONS BY SCOTT
McDOUGALL AND KATE McGUIRE
PHOTOGRAPHS BY JESS KOPPEL

SOMA
san francisco

First published in Great Britain 1998 by Pavilion Books Limited. North American edition published 1998 by SOMA Books, by arrangement with Pavilion Books Limited.

SOMA Books is an imprint of Bay Books & Tapes, Inc., 555 De Haro St., No. 220, San Francisco, CA 94107.

For the Pavilion edition:
Home Economist: Lyn Rutherford
Stylist: Roisin Nield
Editor: Norma Macmillan

For the SOMA edition:
Publisher: James Connolly
Art Director: Jeffrey O'Rourke
Editorial Director: Clancy Drake
North American Editor: Heather Garnos

All measurements should be taken as a point of departure only. The best results come from your own experience.

Vegetarian recipes are marked with the symbol ♥

b.c.e. is an abbreviation of "Before the Common Era".

Library of Congress Cataloging-in-Publication data on file with the Publisher

ISBN 1-57959-004-7

Colour reproduction by Reed Digital, England
Printed and bound in Italy
10 9 8 7 6 5 4 3 2 1

Distributed to the trade by Publishers Group West

CONTENTS

ACKNOWLEDGMENTS

I am indebted to Professor Sogen Hori of McGill University in Toronto, Canada, for helping with the principles of Zen cuisine, and for the verses in the Boiling Up Emptiness sidebar and the Zen Verses sidebar. Although our first introduction was a sad one (he first wrote to my family when his teacher, Kobari Nanrei passed away), I have been greatly enriched through knowing him.

Reverend Kobori was the abbot of Ryokoin of Daitokuji in Kyoto. He was a magnificent representative of his tradition. Without masters like Reverend Kobori, it would be impossible to imagine that a human being could embody gentle peace, steel discipline, and serene compassion. May his students continue to spread the precious message of Zen throughout the world.

PREFACE

The next time you go shopping, take a moment to sit down. Perhaps you'll put your groceries down on a park bench. Or you'll take a minute before you start your car. Or you'll just sit on your front step. Think how you tried to pick your foods and combine them in a graceful way. Think of the many ways your cooking provides for yourself and your family. Think how food is part of a great cycle—from growth to nourishment to recycling of waste—and how you are a part of that circle.

If you can consider all of this, then you're already close to being a Zen cook.

Zen cooking means:

- cooking as a personal spiritual act
- personally selecting foods
- recycling leftovers and waste
- respect for and hospitality toward guests
- an absolutely clean kitchen
- use of the freshest seasonal ingredients
- the ability to cook anywhere in the world with whatever is on hand
- being equally capable of cooking frugally and extravagantly
- using food to enhance health

People who love cooking probably incorporate many of these values already. But these various actions can all be fitted together in a way that makes cooking more than a vocation or profession. Zen makes cooking into a way of life.

Join us and find new approaches to food, and maybe even other aspects of your life, too. In so doing, you may well find yourself agreeing with the famous Zen master Dogen: "Dharma is eating and eating is dharma."

INTRODUCTION

THIS BOOK COMES TO US AS A GIFT. OPENING IT AND USING IT,
WE CAN REALIZE OUR OWN GIFT, THE GIFT OF FOOD, AND THE
BLESSINGS THAT COME TO HAND.

The food we cook, each thing we do, invariably reflects what is in our hearts. When our hearts are preoccupied with "getting it right," we tend to hold back. When we do not hold back, whether we like it or not, we reveal ourselves for the whole world to see. And being willing to be seen unbinds the heart. The old Chinese saying has it that, "If you do not bring out what is in your heart it will lead to frustration, anger, ill will, disease and death. If you bring out what is in your heart it will lead to vitality, warmth, compassion, generosity, good health, and happiness." And one thing in our hearts is the desire to nourish.

Years ago I traveled to Karma Choling, a Tibetan Buddhist meditation center in Barnet, Vermont. A visiting lama gave a lecture extolling the virtue of meditation, describing the meditation hall as an "auspicious" place to practice. He emphasized this point over and over again, so that I began to wonder about people who were not meditating regularly. Did they have any chance at all? So when it came to the time for questions, I asked, "You say the meditation hall is the most auspicious place to be in this life, but somebody has to do the cooking. Somebody has to fix the plumbing. Is there any hope for them?"

The lama smiled. "The meditation hall is the most auspicious place to practice, but if you do work with complete willingness, that is exactly the same thing." He went on to describe a well-known cook who, while he was doing his work serving others, attained all the realizations of those participating in the meditation retreat.

Willingness turns chore to pleasure. Willingness awakens the innate generosity of spirit and kindness of heart that enable us to engage with the things of this world with receptiveness, curiosity, and interest. As Japanese Zen teacher Dogen explained, "Let your mind go out and abide in things. Let things return and abide in your mind."

Willingness is also what enables the cook. Flavors are richer, aromas are more enticing. The everyday burden becomes an adventure. Discovery is possible once again. Life in the kitchen becomes spiritual, and the spirit is freed to engage with things spontaneously and freshly. Let your spirit play, let your hands delight in their activity. When you don't worry about trying to be perfect, you can immerse yourself in the aromas and tastes, the feelings and sensations of being vitally alive and aware of the blessings of this world.

My teacher Suzuki Roshi said, "When you cook, you are not just cooking. You are working on yourself. You are working on others." I invite my frustration, anger, and sorrow; my tenderness, care, and compassion to come into the kitchen with me. This is not the same as giving them free rein to do what they want. If this were so I might hide in a hole in the ground or beat a pillow with my fists. Instead I invite them to join me in cooking. Anger becomes intensity and focus, energy and vigor. Sorrow reaches out to touch and be touched. The distressing emotions are transformed into nourishment.

If you want to meet yourself, renew yourself, integrate yourself, go into the kitchen and start cooking. In the heat of the kitchen your spirit will be distilled as your emotions are transformed into food.

Many people don't know how to cook and use this as an excuse not to cook, while others decide to find out how. Cooking with devotion will transform you and turn you into a source of nourishment for yourself and others. If that's what you want, go for it. People also say, "I don't like cooking." But it's not cooking that's the problem, it's the way we do it. Basic Buddhism teaches that any activity says more about the doer than it does about the activity itself. More accurately these people should say, "I don't like cooking the way I cook." But we can change the way that we do something so that our doing becomes interesting, enjoyable, and engaging. Saying, "I don't like cooking so I'm not going to cook" means that we remain victims of circumstances, prisoners of our likes and dislikes. We empower ourselves by deciding. "I don't like cooking so I will find out how to cook in a way that sustains me." This is to "realize the Way."

Suzuki Roshi said that Buddhists and Taoists would probably eat pretty much the same foods, but with different spirit. His feeling was that the Taoist would put a bit more emphasis on what to eat, the Buddhist on how to eat. Focusing on what to eat, we will study which foods are warming and which are cooling, which are strengthening and which are cleansing. We will observe how we feel when eating various foods at various times. When we work on how to eat we will emphasize gratitude. We bow before receiving food. To bow is to be thankful, and being thankful is to acknowledge that all beings are interconnected and that we receive their support and suste-nance. Gratitude is seasoning, an enzyme that helps us to digest the food.

Food is not just matter. Food is your very being. "Everyday rice and ordinary tea" is said to be the teaching of the buddhas and ancestors. Food is the entire universe. Food is medicine. How will you handle it? What will you do with it? How will you receive it?

Zen: The Art of Modern Eastern Cooking offers both Zen and Taoist teachings, as well as creative recipes filled with a variety of exciting flavors, so it will speak to a large number of people. We won't all cook in the same way or have the same interests. What is important is to appreciate our own gifts, as well as the approach others take.

If we are balanced we find ways to cultivate aspects of ourselves we may have neglected, or to refine the capacities that we already have. We can find ways to bring out the best in ourselves and others, and to bring out the best in the food. This may be warmth and connection, nourishment and friendship, knowledge and reason. If we allow it, our life force will blossom in ways both expected and unexpected.

Zen: The Art of Modern Eastern Cooking offers several approaches to cooking. See if you can find the approach that will suit your own way of cooking, and enhance your way of life. Bon Appetit.

EDWARD ESPE BROWN

ZEN

PART 1

ZEN FLAVORS

Zen is simply everyday life lived with awareness.
When master Baizhang Huaihai (720–814) was
asked about Zen, he replied:

"When you are hungry you eat, when you are thirsty
you drink, when you meet a friend you greet him."

In saying this, he echoed the Chinese philosopher
Mencius: "Tao is near, yet people seek it far away."
For those of us who love cooking and eating, this
makes spirituality no farther away than the bowl in
front of us.

A LIFE OF ATTENTION

ZEN AND TAOISM

When Zen Buddhism came to China, it changed drastically under the influence of Taoism. When Mazu Daoyi declared, in the early part of the eighth century, "If you have a thorough realization of the Taoist philosophy, you can live your daily life, wear your clothes, eat your meals, rear and nourish your inner womb of holiness…," he was referring to the immortal embryo, a spiritual energy Taoists cultivate deep in their abdomens.

Zen masters absorbed Taoist philosophy and made frequent allusions to the Tao. Hanshan Deqing wrote an annotation to the Taoist classic Zhuang Zi *during the Ming dynasty. Nanchuan Puyuan said, "Tao is nothing but the ordinary mind."*

Huineng, the great Sixth Master of Zen (b. 638), said, "The non-dual nature is the real nature…. Eternal and unchanging, we call it the Tao."

Perhaps it's in their mutual celebration of the everyday that Zen and Taoism are closest in spirit. Linji Yixuan aggressively asserted the everyday nature of Zen: "Followers of Tao! Buddhism accepts no artificial methods. It consists solely of doing ordinary things without fuss. Pass stool, make water, put on clothes, eat a meal, sleep when tired…. Don't try to be clever or ingenious. Be ordinary."

Such a down-to-earth philosophy may not be what the public expects of Zen. People associate Zen with perplexing pronouncements and sparse gardens. While Zen does have its complexities and stark spaces, that only makes its practical side more important. Zen has a love of plain hard work and rustic living that can make it attractive to us all.

Indeed, while the austerity of its gardens, the quietness of its meditation, the directness of its paintings, and the simple clarity of its poetry are all wonderful introductions to Zen, it is precisely this practical attitude towards work and living that makes Zen so compelling. Zen sees religious profundity not simply in philosophical inquisitiveness, but in food and cooking as well: "Dharma (ultimate reality)," said Dogen, the master who brought Zen to Japan from thirteenth-century China, "is eating and eating is dharma."

There are numerous schools of Zen throughout the world, each one of which is valid and worthy of the utmost respect. Some Zen schools are opposed to mixing other methods of Buddhism with their own. By contrast, other schools not only encourage visits to other sects of Buddhism, they even encourage exploration of other systems such as Taoism and yoga. The purpose of this book is to look at what is universally meant by Zen —and to enjoy its role in cooking.

Accordingly, Zen teachings from different sources have been utilized, without prejudice whether they are Chinese, Japanese, or otherwise. Also, since Zen and Taoism have had such a history of cross-fertilization, Taoist sources have also been used.

Whether a story, master, or tradition is Zen or Taoist will be noted not for the sake of dividing one system from another, but to avoid perpetuating confusion and fallacies.

Zen has always adapted itself to the country in which it has found itself. It originated in India—the word Zen is a transliteration of the Sanskrit word for meditation—and changed under the influence of Taoism to suit the Chinese culture.

The meeting of Zen with Taoism sparked a centuries-long exchange. Taoism, China's indigenous spiritual tradition, combined meditative practices, nature worship, poetry, and tersely argumentative writings such as *Zhuang Zi*, all of which had a clear impact on Zen. Taoism was also the primary refuge for the eccentrics of China—poets, revolutionaries, painters, alchemists, musicians, warriors, and recluses. This freer approach was the perfect starting point for Zen, which advocated spirituality outside and beyond the scriptures.

Zen means meditation. Tao means the way of all life, a constantly changing flow. Zen begins with the ultimate premise: that all truth is void. It advocates a leap of understanding from that premise. Taoism takes the opposite approach: complete understanding comes only after gradual exploration of lesser truths. Both are adamant that all spirituality is the result of a full and personal lifetime investment.

It is impossible to read any Zen literature without encountering the word Tao. Tao is within Zen and, after the original Buddha, is its most significant source.

When Zen traveled to Japan, it changed according to the needs and outlook of the Japanese. When Zen came to the West, it continued this process of adaptation. The recipes in this book reflect Zen's history of cultural adaptation by including basic Asian dishes and dishes caught in the cusp between East and West, as well as the way of preparing and serving tea, which forms one of Zen's most accessible culinary traditions.

In his famous book, *Instructions to the Cook (Tenzo Kyokun)*, Dogen wrote that only monks wholly intent on seeking the Way (Tao) were qualified to be head cooks. Cooking was a responsibility not to be delegated, not even for the chanting of prayers, because a monk of great concentration was best able to plan, shop for, cook, present, and clear a meal.

Dogen learned about this personal attitude toward cooking while in China. His ship was docked, perhaps waiting clearance for its passengers to disembark, when he met a Chinese monk who had come aboard to buy imported mushrooms. Dogen invited the monk to tea, and, delighting in their religious discussions, pressed the monk to join him for a meal.

The monk declined:

"If I don't oversee tomorrow's offering, it won't be well made."

"Surely there are others in the monastery who can cook? If one cook is missing, will it matter?"

"This is the fulfillment of many years' practice. How could I delegate my responsibility?"

"You could concentrate on meditation and study the words of the ancients instead of working so hard."

The monk laughed. "You don't understand practice, nor do you understand the words of the ancients!"

This spirit of personal practice was made clearer when Dogen visited a monastery. It was a hot day and, as he was crossing the courtyard, Dogen saw the chief cook drying mushrooms in the sun. The monk had no hat to shield his head, his back was as bent as a bow, and his eyebrows were completely white. Seeing how heavy his task was, Dogen gently asked how long the man had been a monk.

"Sixty-eight years."

"Why don't you let someone else do this?"

"Others are not me."

"You are deeply devoted, but the sun is so hot. Why work so hard in the sun? Why not do this work later? "

"If I don't do this now, when should I do it?"

With experiences such as these, Dogen learned of the great tradition of work in Zen temples. Through his writings, that tradition continued through Japanese Zen. It is the spirit of personal labor for all monks, regardless of rank, that sets Zen apart from other monastic traditions. Typically, Zen monks and masters alike will spend a number of weeks repairing walls, tending the gardens, or cooking, before being assigned a new job in rotation with other monks.

These labors are not seen as drudgery: Zen considers that every moment of work holds the possibility of enlightenment. Spiritual insight is possible at any time, as long as a person remains attentive while working. For example, Dogen said:

"Don't lose even one grain of rice. Wash it thoroughly, put it in the pot, light the fire, and cook. View the pot as if it were your own head. See the water as if it were your lifeblood."

We can certainly adapt these ideals to our modern lives. Just as the head cook plans the meal personally, we can do the same. Like the monk on Dogen's ship, we can select our own foods. And as Dogen urged us not to lose one grain of rice, we can cook with the utmost attention, not even lapsing when it comes to disposing of leftovers. Finally, in the cleaning and storing of our implements for the next day, we can gladly prepare for another cycle of cooking.

THE FOUR PRINCIPLES

ONE DAY WITHOUT WORKING, ONE DAY WITHOUT EATING

Buddhist monasteries in India depended on donations and begging for support, and when Zen first came to China, this tradition continued. The late eighth-century master, Baizhang Huaihai, wanted his students to be self-supporting. He radically changed the nature of Zen and monastic life when he instituted the duty of working in the fields. Baizhang retained the practice of begging for alms to encourage humility.

Baizhang himself worked hard in the fields, accepting no privileges as an abbot. Even when he was over eighty years old, he was still working hard. Out of compassion, his students wanted their master to work less, so one day they hid his farming tools.

Baizhang said nothing. But he did not eat that day. Neither did he eat the next day. Thinking that he was angry, his confused students returned his tools. Only then would the master eat again, and his remark became a Zen motto: "One day without working, one day without eating."

During the Song dynasty, other monks besides Dogen traveled from Japan to China for study. In addition to Zen, they returned with art, poetry, medicine, and, most especially, tea. In the ensuing centuries, Zen monks and others refined tea drinking into chanoyu—the tea ceremony.

The tea ceremony celebrates four basic principles, as established by Sen Rikyu *(see page 17)*: respect, harmony, purity, and tranquillity. By adopting these four principles, we can immediately incorporate Zen into our daily cooking.

RESPECT

Zen means respect both for our guests and for the food we eat.

Consideration for our guests begins as we prepare the setting. The garden is meticulously groomed. The room is swept clean. A carefully selected scroll may be hung in an alcove, and a vase of fresh flowers set before it. The tea is of high quality, presented in a precious bowl. At the outset of the gathering, we bow to the guests.

When it comes to the cooking of food, we can apply these same principles. Is the kitchen a clean and calm place? Is the meal artfully served? Do we care for our family and guests? Do we serve them with grace and humility? Does the conversation and interaction over the meal show consideration for others? At the end, is the meal finished in a gentle and meaningful way?

In the temples, no consumption of food takes place until an offering has been made to the gods and the founder of the temple.

Offering food to some higher source before our meals shows gratitude, helps us to think about a world outside ourselves, and reinforces our connection with those who provided for us.

There is also respect for the food itself. Zen does not automatically mean vegetarianism. Certainly, Zen cooks may live in nonvegetarian families, and Zen monks are allowed to eat meat outside the temples. Zen knows that everything we eat is living. Vegetables, fish, poultry, and animals are all alive until we take them for our own consumption. The grain of wheat is really a seed that the plant would otherwise use for its own reproduction. The water we drink is interrupted from its normal cycle to nurture us and cleanse us. Even a mineral like salt, an essential ingredient in our diet, we take from the earth and sea. We interrupt other living processes in order to feed ourselves: our food comes through the sacrifices of others. That is a reality we should respect.

So in all parts of cooking—serving guests, cooking, offering, and eating—let us be respectful. In that solemn awareness, we already have the beginnings of Zen.

PURITY

Purity means cleanliness. Your kitchen and cooking implements must be meticulously clean. In the strictest Zen kitchens, separate knives, chopping boards, and vessels are used for the preparation of vegetables and the preparation of meat. On a religious level, this practice shows respect for these two different types of food. On a practical level, it

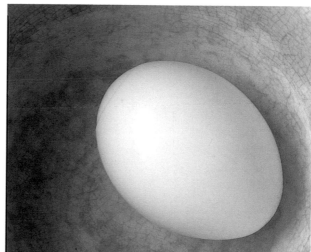

RESPECT   PURITY

HARMONY   TRANQUILLITY

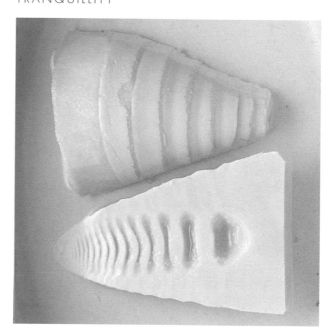

is a sanitary practice to prevent the spread of bacterial contamination.

Purity means freshness. Zen cooking uses the freshest—and therefore most pure—ingredients. Zen cooking begins in the garden or the marketplace, where freshness is measured not by weeks and days but by hours and minutes. Any food begins to change within hours after it's harvested, and every food has an ideal moment of consumption. By taking advantage of those times, we can enhance our respect for food and improve our health.

Purity means letting the natural flavors of the food come through. If you have the freshest of ingredients, it is not necessary to smother them in heavy sauces. Select the food and cook it lightly with seasoning that enhances rather than obscures, and you will have the best-tasting and most healthful food possible.

Purity means clarity of flavor. When you eat such a dish, it smells fresh, and its taste releases a fragrance in your mouth that no sauce or artificial seasoning could ever impart to food.

Purity means naturalness. A Zen cook doesn't use artificial ingredients. A Zen cook doesn't use heavily processed food. A Zen cook doesn't use food that has been imported from far away. A good cook can cook year-round with the ingredients that grow in the garden. A Zen cook knows everything about the ingredients used. In a sense, he or she has already formed a personal relationship with natural produce either by growing it or personally selecting it.

Artificial and processed foods divorce us from this relationship.

Purity means that the cook has a pure and open attitude. Someone who understands that cooking begins with the selection of the ingredients, someone who respects those ingredients enough to let their natural flavors stand alone, someone who is confident enough in his or her cooking to cook lightly and to present a dish in all its natural color, is a person who embraces purity.

HARMONY

Cooking is a social activity. Whether you are cooking for a family, school, or temple, you are cooking for others. Even if you are cooking for yourself, you undoubtedly had to buy at least some of your meal, and your food is in some way touched by others as well—even the waste from your cooking will affect others.

Harmony in cooking means that we are aware of for whom we are cooking and what they need. If the people for whom we are cooking are ill or out of balance, we cook to help or even heal them. If the people for whom we are cooking need a meal to facilitate friendships, we can arrange meals to do that too.

Harmony also means that the way we combine foods makes sense. Here, we have to blend foods with a complex mix of priorities. Much of Zen cooking features dishes with more than one ingredient. We don't simply grill a steak. We slice up the meat and combine it with vegetables. We don't simply have a soup of plain broth. That broth

is made up of many different foods, and it serves as the matrix for a large number of other ingredients. Yet, we can't arbitrarily combine foods either. The Zen cook utilizes the Taoist philosophy of combining foods. Through the understanding of yin and yang and the five element theories, food is combined to make complete and harmonious dishes. A dish where the foods have been combined harmoniously means that the health of those who eat it will also be harmonious.

Harmony is further expressed through the presentation of each dish. Harmony in cooking means that the colors of the foods combine as gracefully as the flavors. A dish that is a delight to the eyes and the nose will be welcomed by the diners. A Zen cook uses all the skill of a painter to combine the colors, forms, and patterns of the food. Such considerations will play a part in how the foods are cut, how they are combined, and then how they are arranged on the plate.

Harmony applies to our relationship with our environment. The Zen cook is constantly aware of the seasons. If the weather is cold, warming dishes and hearty portions are called for. If the time is hot, then cooling foods and smaller portions are needed. Environmental harmony also means ecological responsibility. What do we do with the leftovers? How do we recycle the water we use to wash our vegetables? How do we recycle our cuttings? How do we avoid polluting the waters? Composting, feeding livestock, utilizing our waste so that it is blended back into nature— all show our willingness to live lightly and responsibly in this world.

TRANQUILLITY

When we eat, let us eat in a quiet spirit. Let us think about the food that has been sacrificed to sustain us. Let us take in the healthy nourishment it offers. Let us contemplate the wonderful way it looks, with bright colors in carefully selected vessels. If we are in a temple, perhaps there will be no talk at all, but if there is conversation, then let it be congenial and calm.

Japanese tea houses, Zen temples, and Zen gardens all inspire great serenity. Simply sitting in a tea room and participating in a tea ceremony instills great calm. The sixteenth-century warlords Oda Nobunaga and Toyotomi Hideyoshi participated in the tea ceremony even in the midst of war. The tea room was supposed to be a place removed from the cares of worldly life, where all participants were viewed without rank. For the time that the participants were in the tea room, the cares of the world—even of war and the ruling of a state—were put aside. Likewise, our kitchens and dining rooms should be spaces of great calm.

This peace is one of the great gifts of Zen. Strife and competition mark many of our activities. Although our endeavors in the world are sometimes no less contentious than those of Nobunaga and Hideyoshi, it is worthwhile to try to make our meals calm events in otherwise turbulent days. If we can find the meditative serenity of Zen during each meal, then we are not far from finding it in all other parts of our lives as well.

SEN RIKYU

Sen Rikyu is the most famous and influential figure in the history of Japanese tea. His father was a wealthy merchant from Sakai, and probably exposed Rikyu to fine pottery and other implements used in tea-making. In his youth, Rikyu studied with two tea masters, one of whom taught him an imperial style of tea-making, and the other of whom advocated the wabi (rustic and simple) style of tea-making. He was initiated into Buddhism at Nanshuji temple, and also eventually studied at Daitokuji.

He rose to the position of tea master for the military dictator Oda Nobunaga. After Nobunaga's death, he entered the service of his successor, Toyotomi Hideyoshi. In 1585, he assisted Hideyoshi at a tea gathering for Emperor Ogimachi held at the Imperial Palace. It was on that occasion that the emperor gave him the Buddhist lay name Rikyu Koji.

Rikyu brought chanoyu to its perfection, transforming it into a way of life. He began to use very tiny, rustic tearooms, such as the two-mat tearoom called Taian, which can still be seen today at the Myokian temple near Kyoto. He encouraged the use of raku tea bowls, to move tea away from its obsession with expensive Chinese pottery. He created flower containers, tea scoops, and lid rests of bamboo, and he took ordinary objects from everyday life and incorporated them into the tea ceremony.

Hideyoshi was not only a great general, he was also a patron of the arts and a tea fanatic. Even during military campaigns, he took time out for Rikyu to prepare his tea. For reasons unclear to this day, Hideyoshi accused the master of treason, and ordered Rikyu's death. Rikyu withdrew to his tea room at his Jurakudai residence in Kyoto, made a last bowl of tea, and wrote two poems, including this one, before committing ritual suicide.

A life of seventy years,
Strength spent to the very last,
With this, my jeweled sword,
I kill both masters and Buddhas.
I carry yet
One article I have gained,
The long sword
That now at this moment
I hurl to the heavens.

There are many stories about Rikyu that have gained the stature of myth. Here are three:

Hideyoshi heard that Rikyu's garden was filled with morning glories, and he announced his wish to see them. When he arrived the next morning, he was furious to discover that there was not a single flower to be seen. When he stepped into the tea room, there was a single perfect morning glory.

On his way to a chanoyu gathering given by his son, Rikyu noticed that one stepping stone was slightly higher than the others, and mentioned this to his companion. His son overheard him, and, during the tea ceremony, stole away to lower the stone, sprinkling water to conceal his work. When his father walked out, however, he noticed immediately.

A tea master from Rikyu's home town owned a highly prized tea caddy. He invited Rikyu to tea, but Rikyu made no sign of having noticed the caddy. Upset that the great Rikyu had not approved of his treasure, the owner broke it to pieces. A friend later collected the pieces and glued them back together. This second tea master invited Rikyu to tea. Immediately, Rikyu asked, "Isn't this the same caddy I saw some time ago? Repaired as it is, it has really turned into a piece of wabi (rustic, frugal—the ideal of chanoyu)." The friend was pleased and returned the now Rikyu-approved caddy to its original owner.

ZEN AND HEALTH

Cooking with awareness also means understanding the nutritional aspects of what we eat. While Zen neither denies nor glorifies the body, it does advocate well-being, as long as it isn't sought as an end in itself. Achieving this well-being means to eat seasonally, selecting the highest-quality foods, and combining them judiciously.

Each season offers produce that is appropriate both to our health and our spirit, and coincidentally, this will also be the most reasonably priced. The heat of summer needs cooling foods—just at the time when melons and peaches are best. The dry cold of winter needs moistening and warming foods—just at the time when squashes and carrots are best. Thus, Zen cooking keeps us integrated with the cycle of nature.

All foods should be personally selected for quality. Whether you grow your own food or buy it, make a decision about each vegetable and fruit, every sack of grain and piece of meat. Does the food look and smell good? Will it make a good contribution to the meal you have in mind? Will the colors blend well? Will the flavors be harmonious? Will the food enhance the health of those who eat it? Will the food impart some extra blessing from the season or place from which it came?

If we can eat the best of what nature offers us at any moment, it is easy to see how there will be immediate benefits to our bodies. Further benefits can come to us if we know more about which foods to eat and when to eat them.

Zen's knowledge of health originated

with ancient Taoist dietary practices. This tradition was built on a long search for immortality, beginning in China as early as the Zhou dynasty (1122–225 b.c.e.). By the third century b.c.e., Emperor Qin Shihuang—who ordered the building of the Great Wall of China, and regulated the script, monetary system, weights and measures, roads, and many other details of the society—had become obsessed with trying to live forever. He invited a constant stream of Taoist alchemists (fangshi, literally "recipe masters") to his court as he searched for the compounds of the elixir of immortality.

The emperor also believed that a legendary mushroom of immortality existed. He sent one thousand men and one thousand maidens beyond his kingdom, with orders to bring the mushroom back. Many of these searchers even set sail over the oceans. It is said that some of them landed on what would eventually became Japan and, not having found the mushroom, chose to stay rather than return to face the prospect of imperial punishment.

After Qin Shihuang's time, the interest in physical immortality evolved into more logical and effective methods. Instead of ingesting mercury, lead, and gold, people used herbs such as ginseng. Instead of trying to live forever, the Taoists concluded that a long and healthy life was a worthy enough goal. Most of the Taoists turned to preventative medicine and sound dietary practices, and this is still the tradition today.

The Taoist ideal of health means harmony with Tao (the Way). Taoists feel that all peo-

ple would live better if they would simply live according to this great Way. They apply this ideal in spiritual matters, political matters, and matters of diet in equal measures: for a Taoist, the normally perceived dichotomies of mind and body, secular and spiritual, human being and nature, are mere continuums within Tao. Eating is as helpful in harmonizing with the Way as is philosophy and meditation.

Zen underwent centuries of cross-fertilization with Taoism. Zen gives us compassion, devotion, and a wonderful aesthetic. Looking through Zen back into Taoism can give us many more principles for good health through diet. Here are further ways to follow the Taoist ideas of diet:

EAT SEASONALLY. Summer, for example, is hot. Cooling foods—salads, fruit, and light fare—are in order. Eat less meat, avoid alcohol, and eat foods that will help moisten the body, such as celery, cucumber, melons, and so on. Autumn is a time of transition, when the lingering effects of summer's heat have to be dispelled. At the same time, cold and dryness begin to affect the body, and so the cook knows how to dispel any toxicity of the departing hot season and begins to serve foods that will prepare the body for the coming cold. The Taoists permit more meats in this season to prepare for winter, and to counter the dryness of autumn, they eat fruits such as dates, figs, pears, and apples. Winter requires foods that are hearty and will heat the body. Stews, heavy meats, and root vegetables become the emphasis

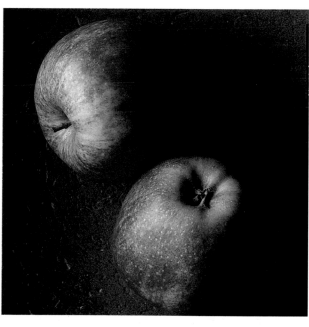

SPRING   AUTUMN

SUMMER   WINTER

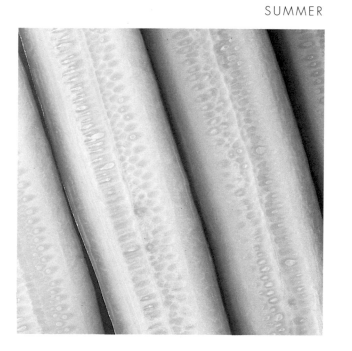

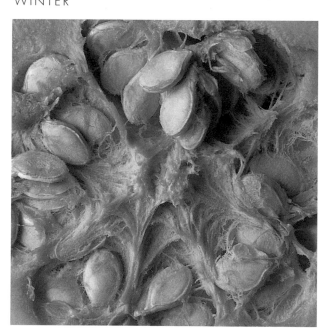

RICE MILK FOR ENLIGHTENMENT

The story of Buddha is a long and beautiful one, filled with color and poetry. Fragments of this biography exist partly in Sanskrit, and partly in Tibetan. The following brief sketch focuses on the role of nourishment in his life.

Buddha is the name for a being who has reached enlightenment. There have been many Buddhas in the past, and there will be many more in the future. The actual person we commonly call Buddha lived in Northern India in the sixth century b.c.e. He was born a prince and named Siddarta.

A great seer predicted that the prince would become a great sage who would liberate humanity from delusion. This distressed Siddarta's royal father greatly. Unwilling to see his son become a wandering renunciate, he decreed that the prince should be exposed to neither ugliness nor suffering. Further, when the prince was of age, he married him to a beautiful woman.

Whenever Siddarta went forth from the palace, all cripples and old people were sent away, and the highway was made beautiful. But on three successive occasions, the gods put an old man, a diseased man, and a corpse onto the road. Each time the shocked prince turned to his chariot driver, who explained that there were aging, illness, and death in the world. Siddarta saw the earth being broken by the plowmen, saw the plants and grasses destroyed, saw insects and small animals die under the plow, and saw the farmers themselves aging and straining to work in the dust and blazing sun.

Eventually, Siddarta left the palace and became an ascetic. Initially, he sought to reach spiritual liberation by denying his body. Over the course of six years, he wasted away to half his weight, but finally realized that the inward calm he sought could only be achieved if physical strength was constantly replenished. He understood that proper nourishment was necessary to perceive the dharma.

At this point, the gods caused the daughter of a cowherd to happen by the weak and crawling ascetic. She helped him up the river bank, and offered him a rich rice milk. This gave him the strength he needed to accomplish his enlightenment.

in this season. Taoists rely primarily on fish and chicken, but will also eat red meats, venison, and even snake. They will also add wine to their diet, to stimulate the body and counter the cold. Spring requires foods that are stimulating and neutral, like simply cooked vegetables and fish rather than heavy meats and spicy foods. Weather is variable in the spring, so the foods must strengthen the body for the unpredictable climate. Spring also means that the excesses of the winter must be dispelled, and the body fortified again. Even when weather conditions are seemingly contrary to the season, the Taoist eats according to the day. If the season is technically summer but it is cold and windy, then a Taoist eats to counter cold and wind. A Taoist is flexible, and makes decisions based on the moment.

EAT A LARGE VARIETY OF FOODS EACH DAY. Limited variety can eventually lead to diseases of dietary imbalance. Meat is permissible, but is useful more in cold weather than warm. It is best to eat it sparingly. Meat should act more as an accent and flavoring to a meal than a primary ingredient.

IT IS FAR BETTER TO EAT FOUR OR FIVE SMALL MEALS A DAY THAN ONE OR TWO LARGE, HEAVY MEALS. This avoids strain on the digestive system and allows you to maintain your energy evenly throughout the day.

MAINTAIN A BALANCE BETWEEN THE LARGE RANGE OF FOODS YOU EAT. Overconsumption of some foods can lead to problems. For example, a little spicy and peppery food can counteract dampness, but too much of it can irritate the stomach. Likewise, overeating and eating too many rich and oily foods can produce symptoms of heartburn, ulcers, and internal bleeding.

ALL FOOD SHOULD BE CLEAN AND WHOLE. During the centuries when the Taoist diet was formed, there were many cases of unsanitary food handling and preparation. The Taoists were the primary group of people who advocated sanitary eating conditions. They advised that all water be boiled, for example, and we can adapt that principle for our times by always drinking filtered, if not boiled, water. Most foods are eaten cooked, another sanitary practice. Raw foods like fruit should be ripe or fully grown, washed well, and peeled, unless one knows with certainty that the fruit was grown under sanitary conditions.

COOKING SHOULD BE THOROUGH, BUT SHOULD NOT DEPLETE THE FOOD OF ITS NUTRIENTS. The freshness of the food, its qi, or vitality, must always be retained.

AT EACH MEAL, EAT AT LEAST THREE DIFFERENT VEGETABLES. One approach is to combine one green, one red, and one yellow vegetable at each meal. Another approach is to "eat a rainbow"—making each meal as colorful as possible is an intuitive and artistic way to ensure diversity.

EAT A VARIETY OF GRAINS. But make sure they are well cooked and moist to avoid digestive problems and to avoid robbing the body of moisture.

FRUIT IS THE IDEAL DESSERT AFTER EVERY MEAL. A minimum of one or two fruits should be eaten each day.

SOY MILK CAN BE CONSUMED ON A DAILY BASIS. For those who are lactose intolerant, dairy products should be avoided. Those who can consume dairy products should be aware that dairy can increase mucus secretions and nasal congestion, so intake should be monitored accordingly.

DRINK ENOUGH WATER. This should be about 8 cups of pure water, drunk gradually throughout the day. The Taoists believe that sufficient hydration is important. Liquid forms the basis of all food, which is why soups are so emphasized in the diet.

AVOID ICED DRINKS, EVEN WHEN THE WEATHER IS HOT. Cold drinks are believed to inhibit digestion and shock the system.

TEA IS GOOD, BUT AVOID DRINKING IT TO EXCESS. Being a tea connoisseur was considered essential to being a good cook and a good Taoist. Taoist studies on this important subject include Lu Yu's *Tea Classic*. About one pot of tea at each meal is right.

BE MODERATE IN ALCOHOL CONSUMPTION. Wine is useful in cold climates, and a Taoist will often drink one serving in the evening during the winter. But do not drink wine to excess—better to avoid it altogether. To a Taoist, overindulgence, like any other type of excess, is to be scrupulously avoided.

EAT AS MUCH AS YOU NEED, BUT DO NOT OVEREAT. Share what you have, and recycle what you do not use. Never waste. Eat both for pleasure and for health, and be moderate at all times.

WHEN YOU EAT, BE AWARE OF WHERE THE FOOD CAME FROM. A well-known aphorism is: "When you drink water, think of its source." Know the source of your food, and remember that you are but one point in a full cycle.

MODERATE EXERCISE, A PEACEFUL DISPOSITION, AND FRESH AIR ARE JUST AS IMPORTANT TO DIGESTION AND METABOLISM AS THE FOOD YOU EAT.

THE COURSES OF A TAOIST BANQUET

There are many legends about the fabulous banquets that Taoists would prepare. Buried in the fascinating folklore of these tales is the lesson of how the different courses followed each other to yield the maximum health benefits to the diners. Eventually, these ideas of different courses came to influence all the ten major schools of Chinese cooking.

Here are the eleven courses of a traditional Taoist banquet, with an explanation of the role each one played in the overall meal:

1. Pickled or vinegary dishes (such as jellyfish): to stimulate the digestive system for the meal ahead.

2. Vegetables, tofu, or other neutral foods: to calm the system and neutralize the body.

3. Meats, fried foods, spicy foods: yang nature foods to stimulate and energize the body.

4. Tonic soups such as shark's fin or soups made with medicinal herbs: to build vitality.

5. Stir-fried foods: to balance the wetness of the preceding soup course.

6. White fish: nutritious but neutral for the body.

7. Vegetable dishes: to neutralize the yang nature of the meats and tonic soups.

8. Mushroom soups: to cleanse the digestive system.

9. Rice or noodles: to fill up the diner.

10. Fruits: cooling, cleansing, and sweet.

11. Teas: different teas were used to stimulate or calm the body according to any final needs of the banquet and the diners.

QI

All of Taoism's interest in health can be centered on the concept of qi (pronounced "chee"), commonly translated as breath. While that definition is accurate, the connotations of this word are much greater than mere respiration.

Qi means energy: for example, if a person is frequently ill, then that person's qi is surely weak. Qi is the moral force of a person: when a person of great charisma is nearby, people speak of feeling the very qi of that person. Qi is life force: a person of great will is said to have great qi. Qi is also a sign of artful skill: a calligrapher's work will show qi. A great cook's dishes will be fragrant—they will have "wok qi."

On a grand scale, qi is also the living and eternal force animating the entire universe. The weather, for example, is called "ky qi." Metaphysically speaking, qi is also the force that makes the planets turn and the stars move. It is hard to overestimate the degree to which the Taoists view the personal qi as being interconnected with the cosmic qi. The Taoists strongly believe that microcosm and macrocosm are all one and the same.

How does a person come to have qi? At birth, there will be qi that comes from the mother and father. Much of the remainder of one's qi comes from the combination of the body's hormones, the essence of food, and air that is breathed in. This produces qi in the body.

The Taoists speak of each person as possessing three treasures: jing—hormones, blood, and all other biochemical components of the body; qi—breath, energy, and life force; and shen—intellect and spirit. Jing produces qi, qi produces shen. Therefore, the Taoists declare that without jing, there is no qi. Without qi there is no shen. And without shen, there is no possibility of realizing one's spirituality.

For the Taoists, spiritual realization is a state of being that literally involves the entire person on all physical, mental, and spiritual levels. A Taoist would not stop short of saying that without proper diet, jing is compromised. Therefore, qi is diminished and then shen is also weakened. In short, without proper physical nourishment, there is no proper spirituality.

A Zen cook therefore lets qi rule during all phases of cooking. Good food has qi. The more fresh and vital any food is, the more qi it has. Food that is of poor quality or is overly processed has little qi. It only makes sense to prepare and eat foods that exude life force, so that the qi of those who eat the food will be augmented. In the kitchen, you can learn to sense qi. While you are preparing the food, the smells should be fresh and distinct. The vegetables should be firm and filled with their juices. The meats should have clear colors and smells. When you cut your food, there should be texture and firmness.

During cooking, use all your senses. What you are measuring is qi. Use sight to time your cooking by the change in colors, so the qi is not driven away by overcooking. Use every sound—boiling bubbles, sizzling grill, bursting stir-fry—to hear the sound of life. Use taste during cooking, to discern balance and harmony. Use touch, to judge whether ingredients are in proper proportion to one another, and whether something is done. Use smell, to know when the qi of a dish is full and bursting from the pot. If you can learn to judge the qi of a dish, your health and the health of all around you will be greatly enhanced.

COMBINING ZEN AND TAOISM IN CONTEMPORARY COOKING

It's easy to see how much Zen and Taoism have in common. Looking at the spiritual nature of cooking from these two closely related points of view can be highly beneficial. From Zen, we can borrow the practice of attention, reverence, aesthetics, and the four principles of respect, harmony, purity, and tranquillity. From Taoism, we can borrow the practice of dietary balance and benefit from its assertion that physical health is a valuable prelude to spiritual practice. In the end, what counts is that the Zen and Taoist ways of life extend the actual cooking and enjoyment of food.

We are always looking for ways to maintain the vitality of our cooking. From the parent looking for another creative way to keep the children interested in their meals, to the restaurateur looking for a new way to attract patrons, we all look back into the past for inspiration. Interest in health, spirituality, attractive presentation, and the pure flavor of good cooking are ever at the forefront. Zen and Taoism have much to offer, and have already greatly influenced contemporary cooking.

When nouvelle cuisine was followed by Japanese-influenced presentations, contemporary cooking began an exploration into the combining of Eastern and Western cuisines. Cooks unknowingly adopted practices with roots in Zen and Taoism. Certainly, the sensitive presentation of food as practiced in kaiseki cooking has had a great impact. And every time a chef borrows from Chinese cooking, he or she is borrowing from a large body of knowledge heavily influenced by Taoist theories. In our ongoing search through the past, why not study the systems as a whole? While they lend themselves to piecemeal borrowing, it is certainly much more valuable to see the whole, and to understand how cooking has always been seen as an activity that involves a whole person and a whole life.

BOILING UP EMPTINESS

This famous Zen verse from the Zenrin Kushu (Zen Forest Verse Collection), *compiled by Toyo Eicho Zenji and reprinted in 1894, contains everything that we need to remember about Zen, Taoism, and eating.*

> *Last night, I boiled up emptiness*
> *And toasted the sugar pot to pieces.*
> *I covet not the Queen Mother's peaches*
> *Having already had the jujube of immortals.*
> *I spit out wild fox drool*
> *And take another drink of belly-pacifying potion.*

Night evokes the quiet solitude of meditative practice. With metaphors of boiling and a pot, there is also a reference to Taoist alchemy. "Emptiness" here refers to the ultimate Zen concept of reality. This emptiness is not a nihilistic vacuum. Rather, it is a state where no distinctions and therefore no contradictions exist. This is not a simple thing to comprehend. Indeed, the understanding of emptiness often requires years of experience.

The Queen Mother is the highest goddess in the Taoist pantheon. She has a garden where peaches of immortality grow. One bite of these peaches extends a person's life by ten thousand years. The Queen Mother holds lavish banquets at which these peaches are eaten as the main course.

The jujube of the immortals is a reference to the elixir of immortality. Taking this elixir will again extend one's lifespan. The verse makes reference to the fact that a Zen practitioner already possesses the secret of "immortality."

A wild fox symbolizes a person who knows Zen only intellectually, and lacks any true experience in it. The saliva of a wild fox represents a vicious poison. What is important is to experience both cooking and spirituality for ourselves, rather than relying on outside sources. Then we will find that we already have the belly-pacifying potion.

GETTING STARTED

It is no exaggeration to say that one of the most radical spiritual acts you can make is to cook your own food. If you know how to cook, you will never be hungry. No matter where you go in the world, you will be self-sufficient. You will be able to partake not only in the actual food of any place, but, because you will take your food from the earth and you will fit in with the seasons of your surroundings, you will always have a way of integrating yourself with time and place. You will be aware of the cycles of existence in a most enjoyable and palpable way. You will always have a way of centering yourself, for to cook in the Zen way is to cook meditatively. Finally, you will be able to control your body, mind, and spirit by controlling the types of food you put into your body; if you can maintain balance in your diet, you will go a long way towards maintaining balance in the rest of your life too. All this is Zen.

If you want to begin the exciting process of Zen cooking, try the following:

CLEAN YOUR KITCHEN AND MAKE IT READY FOR COOKING. Purity is one of the central tenets of Zen cooking.

BUILD YOUR ZEN PANTRY. Choose some of the basic foods and condiments you will need. Certainly, rice, a variety of noodles, soy sauce, rice wine, rice vinegar, ginger, garlic, salt, pepper, tea, and filtered water are essential. As you experiment with the recipes, you will naturally add more ingredients.

EQUIP YOUR KITCHEN. The two most basic implements for Asian cooking are a cleaver and a wok. In a sense, a good Zen wanderer could cook a meal with little more than a knife and pot. Some simple herbs and vegetables, fresh spring water, and a fire in the mountains might be all that a person needed. While we need to preserve that spirit of simplicity, a well-equipped kitchen will have a good cleaver and wok, as well as many other kinds of equipment.

CLEAVER AND KNIVES

If you can only have one cleaver, buy one that feels fairly heavy in your hand. See if the balance is the way you like it. Unlike Western-style knives, the weight of the knife is centered in the blade for more forceful cutting. If you can afford more than one cleaver, get light, medium, and heavy cleavers at the very least. The lighter one is for cutting vegetables, the middle one is for slicing meats, and the heaviest one is for splitting bones. A pair of medium-weight cleavers is used, one in each hand, to chop rapidly and finely.

Even with food processors available, cooks still use knives. Hand-cut food varies slightly in size. Each piece will therefore cook differently, imparting a variety of textures and flavors that is impossible to achieve by machine.

Cooks use all the parts of a cleaver: the flat of the blade can be used to crush garlic (a simple way to peel the garlic is to put it on your chopping board and quickly smash it with the flat of your cleaver; this will break the clove and make it very easy to peel) or to quickly spread out dough for dumpling wraps. The back of the blade is used to pound meat for tenderizing. The butt of the handle is used as a pestle to crush salted soy beans for black bean sauce. And the corner of the blade closest to the handle can be used to puncture cans.

As versatile as the cleaver may be, a variety of Western knives are useful as well. Chef's, boning, and paring knives would be helpful, and other knives can be added as needed. There are times, such as when peeling chestnuts or cutting seafood for sashimi, where a specialized knife is best. These knives should stay perfectly level when balanced on your index finger in a normal grip position.

All knives should be kept well honed and rust free. Learn how to use sharpening stones. The exercise of sharpening is in itself a spiritual act.

CHOPPING BLOCK

Using a knife in a kitchen is impossible without a good chopping block. Here, you have a choice between an end-grain butcher's block or laminated flat-grain boards. The wood should be neutral and hard, kept meticulously clean, never left standing in water, and oiled periodically with mineral oil. Keep a scraper blade on hand so that water can be quickly removed from the surface after washing. Stand the board upright along the long grain while it dries. If the wood gets too rough from repeated cutting, or if it becomes stained, it can be resurfaced with

PRINCE WEN HUI'S COOK

Zhuang Zi was the author of many pivotal Taoist texts. We know he was a considerable influence on early Zen thinkers because many of them translated or made comments on his work, and masters throughout the ages have quoted him in their teachings. He gives us this parable.

Prince Wen Hui watched his cook carving up an ox. With sensitive movements of his hand, deft heaves of his shoulders, strong footwork, and rapid thrusts of his knife, the cook's movements were as graceful as those of a dancer's.

The prince praised him by saying, "How wonderfully you have mastered your art."

Respectfully, the cook laid down his knife and replied, "Your servant cares most about Tao, which goes beyond mere art. I follow the natural grain, letting the knife find its way through the many hidden openings. I take advantage of what is there and never need to touch a ligament or tendon.

"A good cook changes his knife once a year. A bad one who hacks must change his once a month. Although I have used my knife for over nineteen years, it remains as sharp as it first came from the whetstone.

The blade's edge has no thickness. There are many spaces between the joints wide enough through which a blade of no thickness can pass. Even when I come to a difficult joint, I look carefully and work slowly. Then, with but a slight movement of my knife, I can cut an entire ox open. After that, I need only wipe my knife clean and put it away."

"Wonderful!" exclaimed the Prince. "From my cook's words, I have learned the secret of life."

a plane or steel brush. Don't use sandpaper, as the abrasives can become embedded in the pores of the wood.

Don't use your knives or boards for anything but cooking. If you want to be completely fastidious and orthodox, use separate implements for cooking with meat and for cooking with vegetables.

WOKS AND PANS

The wok is central to Asian cooking. It is a thin, nearly hemispherical pan, with either a single long handle or two loop handles. Woks are made as small as 12 inches across, and as large as 3 feet in diameter. A basic wok kit would require at least the wok, a cover, and a long spatula (long enough to reach the center of the wok while keeping your hand outside the circumference). A new wok should be seasoned by thoroughly washing it, and then wiping it with oil before heating it for about 20 minutes.

Supplementary items that are very useful include a long sieve (usually woven brass wire on a bamboo handle), a large ladle the same length as the spatula, stacking bamboo steamers smaller than the diameter of the wok, a semicircular draining rack if you deep-fry, and, for cleaning, a bamboo scrubbing brush and a metal scouring brush.

If you do not have a wok, useful substitutes are a large Dutch oven or flameproof casserole (which will allow longer, higher heating) or a 12-inch frying pan. In addition to a wok, you will need a variety of sauté pans, saucepans, and stockpots for the recipes in this book.

Woks and pans with vastly improved nonstick surfaces are quite useful. If you have these pans, you will be able to use far less oil. Oil is then used to season rather than to prevent sticking. Food cooked in a nonstick pan will be more evenly cooked, sometimes more moist, and will have more distinct flavors. Naturally, if you use such a nonstick pan, you should use only wooden or nylon implements specifically intended for use with these surfaces.

CHOOSE YOUR FOODS

You will need to obtain your food either by growing it yourself or by going to the market. If you are growing some or all of your food yourself, you are lucky and accomplished. What better way to understand the cycles of nature than to raise your own produce? However, it is likely that you will have to go to the market to buy at least some of your food.

If your community has a farmers' market, then that is the best place to start. By regularly frequenting your local farmers' market, you will accomplish several goals of Zen cooking. You will eat in season, for the farmers obviously bring the best of their harvest to market. You will know where your food comes from—a good way to connect yourself spiritually with the growth cycle. You will probably be able to buy organic foods, which are far better for your health than artificially processed foods. And you will be obtaining your food yourself. Remember, this is where the cooking starts: in selecting the foods you will eat. When you walk around a farmers' market, your eyes will take in all the varied colors of the available foods. You will begin to plan meals in your mind. You will become excited over a food just brought to market, and how fresh and vital it is. You will learn about new foods, and will be likely to explore. You will learn to pick the freshest foods by having several stalls for comparison, and you will learn to shop frugally, too.

Shopping in a farmers' market is to open your entire being to selecting the right foods. As soon as you go into a good market, you will know before even looking that the food is good: you will be able to smell the fragrances and aromas of fresh food. Your eyes will roam freely and revel in the variety. You will have to walk, and breathe, and move, and wander. You will touch your food, turn it over, make sure it is of sufficient quality to put into your body. In time, your fingers will become sensitive, and a touch will be all you need to understand the proper firmness of fruit, or the texture of vegetables. Above all, you will be exercising your perception, your creativity, and your understanding. Out of an entire crate of strawberries, you will pick a certain basket. Out of the entire box of mushrooms, you will select only a few.

If you don't have a farmers' market in your community, or if you must go outside the farmers' market for other ingredients, then try to come as close as possible to the Zen of shopping. Look for specialty shops where you can develop a good relationship with the shopkeeper. Ask which foods are freshest, and listen to any advice about storing or preparing the food. Know where your food comes from. The worst thing you can do is to blindly grab food, or accept prepackaged products where you can neither see, smell, nor touch the whole food.

If you have the chance to shop in an Asian market, then look for one with plenty of fresh fruit and vegetables. The turnover should be rapid. In most Asian markets, the stock must be replenished several times a day, and that is good. There should be live fish, and the fish that are on display must have shining eyes, red gills, and glistening skin. There should be no foul smells in the air. Meat should be lean and clean in color. Look also for a market that has a large stock of condiments, grains, soy products, and pickled items. In a large city, you should be able to find Chinese, Japanese, Vietnamese, Thai, and other Asian markets, and as you become familiar with them, you should be able to find all the ingredients you will need.

You need not be intimidated by such seemingly "foreign" markets. Everyone understands the desire to eat. In markets all over Asia and in Asian markets throughout the rest of the world, people of all races and backgrounds are welcome, and there are frequent attempts to bridge the language barriers in the pursuit of good food.

ZEN

PART 2

CLASSIC FLAVORS

There are a certain number of dishes that are important for any Zen cook to know. If you can cook these classic dishes, you will never be hungry. These dishes are inexpensive and use ingredients found the world over. You will also be of great service to others: whether you find yourself cooking for a few family members or close friends, or for a large gathering, you will be able to feed people. Finally, these basic dishes are useful because they allow you to improvise. If you can stir-fry cabbage, you can certainly stir-fry spinach, broccoli, carrots, or any other vegetables. If you know how to cook a noodle soup with fish, then you can certainly cook it with any meat or with vegetables alone. So much of cooking, like Zen, lies not in the specifics of the technique, but in the experience that brings understanding. Once you know how to cook, you can see beyond the ingredients to the essence of the meal itself.

VEGETARIAN STOCK

Stock is an important dish to master for two reasons: because it is the basis for soups and because so many dishes use stock as part of the cooking process. While canned broth and "fresh" stocks are available, and useful when time is short, the Zen approach is to make your own. You will then know exactly what went into your stock and, because soup stock can be made with bones and vegetable cuttings that might otherwise be thrown away, you will not be wasting anything.

Try to use all your stock within 3 days. Some cooks freeze their stock, sometimes even freezing it in ice cube trays so that they can use a little at a time. You will have to try this and see if the slight difference in taste is worth the savings in time.

As part of a full meal, soup often functions as a harmonizing element to balance the other dishes. For example, if there are many fried foods at the table, a soup with cooling vegetables such as watercress or winter melon can lend balance.

You can make your own vegetarian stock by saving the vegetable cuttings from your other food preparations. If you don't have enough right away (at least 2 pounds), freeze the vegetable cuttings you do have in an airtight container until you have enough to make stock. When you are ready to make it, put the vegetable cuttings in at least 10 cups of water, enough to completely submerge the ingredients. Cover and simmer gently for 2 to 4 hours. The more you reduce the stock, the stronger the taste.

Some cooks like to make stock from only one or two vegetables, often for medicinal reasons. For example, a watercress stock, made by taking one bunch of watercress and simmering for 4 to 6 hours in as much as 10 cups of water, is used to chase away the effects of fever from the body and to moisten the lungs.

For a formal vegetarian stock made from fresh ingredients, try the following recipe. It cooks all the nutrients of the vegetables into the stock. (While it's possible to eat the vegetables, primarily for the fiber, most of the flavor will have gone.) The stock is sweet, clear, and a light jade-yellow. There is purposefully no salt in the recipe: if the stock is used alone, you can add soy sauce for seasoning. If the stock is added to other dishes, the seasoning for those dishes should be enough.

Makes about 10 cups

8 ounces carrots
8 ounces celery stalks with leaves
8 ounces parsnips
1 medium onion
1 ounce fresh ginger
1 ounce Chinese dried red dates
8 cups water

Clean and trim all the vegetables, then roughly chop them. Place all the ingredients in a large stockpot. Cover and bring to a boil. Reduce to a simmer, keeping the lid on, and cook for 1 to 1 1/2 hours. Strain and use immediately in a recipe or set aside.

WATER

There is a famous saying, "When you drink water, think of its source."

Lao Zi urges each of us to be like water: "A person of superior goodness is like water," and goes on to describe a great person as "dwelling in the good earth, with a mind like water." (Dao De Jing, poem 8).

Water is the most basic element; as Lao Zi says, it does not disdain the lowliest of places. Yet it is also one of our greatest spiritual examples. Without complaint, it goes through the cycles of freezing, evaporation, rainfall, running, and pooling. No matter what transformations it goes through, it never loses its essential nature.

Not one of us can do without water—that precious gift that we take into our bodies, and which leaves us after we have used it, to become pure once again. Water is our first food. Isn't it one of the most indispensable parts of exercise, of daily living, and of recovering from illness? It is also the primary ingredient in so many other foods. You may well have noticed how many Asian meals begin with a soup; this gives the body liquid to work with rather than forcing it to liquefy the food during digestion. We also need pure, fresh water to make rice, stews, pickles, and tea.

Ideally, water should be "living" water, drawn directly from a spring or well. If that is impossible, a practical alternative is to use filtered water with as many of the impurities removed as possible. All water used as an ingredient in cooking and for brewing tea should be free of lead, sediment, chlorine, and other pollutants.

A simple test you can use to convince yourself that filtered water really makes a difference is to brew two cups of tea, one cup with tap water and the other cup with pure water. If you look at the tea in white porcelain cups, you are sure to see the difference in color. And if you taste the tea, you will taste a difference as well. In time, you may even find yourself fond of "White Tea," that poor person's drink: simple boiled water.

BASIC DASHI

Dashi is stock prepared from dried kelp and paper-thin shavings of dried bonito tuna. Dashi serves as the base for miso soup, seasoned broth for nimono (see part 4), and as one of the fundamental seasonings used throughout a kaiseki meal. This dashi, derived from kaiseki cooking, is richer in taste than that ordinarily prepared for home cooking, and will yield enough dashi for an entire kaiseki meal. Any leftover dashi can be frozen for up to 2 months.

Dried bonito flakes are usually sold in a box or plastic container. They should be pale pink in color. Instant dashi powder or mix that contains dried sardines and other seasonings is often available, but should be used only as a last resort. Any unused bonito flakes should be stored in an airtight container at room temperature.

The best dried kelp comes from the deep, cold waters of Hokkaido. It is dark green, thick and wide, with curly edges, somewhat resembling dried lasagna noodles. Quality dried kelp is often covered with white natural salts. The powder should not be rinsed off as it adds flavor to the broth. Store in an airtight container.

There are many brands of dried bonito flakes and kelp available at Japanese supermarkets. More often than not, price is an indication of quality. Let your taste and experience be your guide.

Makes at least 10 cups

12 1/2 cups cold water
2 ounces konbu (dried kelp), torn into strips
7 cups loosely packed hana katsuo (dried bonito flakes)

Place all but 1 cup of the water in a stockpot. Add the kelp and gently simmer for 20 minutes. Do not allow the water to come to a boil as this will make the kelp slimy.

Remove the kelp and add the reserved cold water to the stockpot. Gradually add the dried bonito flakes. Let the dashi simmer gently for 5 minutes. The dashi should have a rich, slightly smoky flavor. If the dashi is not strong enough, add more dried bonito.

Strain the dashi through a fine mesh sieve. Do not press the bonito flakes as this will cause the dashi to become cloudy and bitter.

SHIITAKE DASHI [v]

A delicious vegetarian dashi can be prepared using konbu and dried shiitake mushrooms. Dried shiitake mushrooms are available in Japanese and Chinese markets, where they are also called black mushrooms.

A relish called tsukudani can be made from the leftover shiitake and kelp that are strained out of the finished dashi. Slice the mushrooms and kelp into thin strips. Simmer with dark soy sauce, some dashi, a little sake, and a large pinch of sugar until the flavors have been absorbed. Tsukudani is excellent served as an accompaniment to rice.

Makes 10 cups

5 medium dried shiitake mushrooms, rinsed
10 cups cold water
1 ounce konbu (dried kelp)

Soak the mushrooms until soft. Save the soaking water for adding to the stockpot.

Place the water, dried kelp, and mushrooms in a large stockpot. Gently simmer for about 20 minutes, tasting from time to time to see how the flavors are developing. Vegetarian dashi should not taste too strongly of either kelp or shiitake. When the dashi is to your liking, strain through a fine mesh sieve.

CHICKEN STOCK

If you are cooking meals with meat, save bones and vegetable cuttings. You can freeze them in an airtight container until you have enough to make stock. You should have at least 2 pounds of material, as a minimum, to start, but your stockpot should not be more than three-quarters full. Add enough cold water to completely submerge the ingredients. Bring to a boil. Then cover and simmer gently for 2 to 4 hours. Skim foam as needed. The more you reduce the stock, the stronger the taste.

For a more formal and rich stock made from fresh ingredients, try the following recipe.

Serves 6 to 8

A 5- to 6-pound fresh chicken
1 veal or beef knuckle bone, or 1 pig's foot (optional)
2 large carrots, split and cut into 1-inch pieces
2 celery stalks with leaves, coarsely chopped
1 medium onion, cubed
4 slices fresh ginger
6 Chinese dried red dates (optional)
2 ounces zhen pei (dried citrus skin) (optional)
Salt and pepper to taste

Clean the chicken thoroughly, especially in the cavity, removing any extra fat. Place the chicken, either whole or quartered, in a large stockpot and cover with water. Cover and bring to a boil. Reduce to a simmer and skim off the foam.

When the surface is free from foam, stir in the remaining ingredients. Simmer gently, with the lid on, for 2 hours. Turn the chicken two or three times during this period. Remove the chicken from the pot and strain the stock. Use immediately, or allow to cool uncovered and store in a covered glass container in the refrigerator for up to 2 days.

When the chicken is cool, strip the meat into small pieces, discarding skin and bones. Small pieces can be added to some broth dishes, or used in a chicken salad.

ONE CHICKEN, TWO WAYS

Here's a great way to have a chicken for the dinner table and a pot full of stock for use in other dishes. The chicken is cooked over very low heat, allowed to cool, and then carved for serving. The stock is then available for other uses.

Serves 6 to 8

A 5- to 6-pound fresh chicken
2 slices fresh ginger
Salt to taste
Peanut or canola oil (optional)
1 green onion
Cilantro to garnish

Wash the chicken well. Bring a pot of water to a boil. Add the ginger, salt, and chicken. Turn the flame down low and simmer for 30 to 40 minutes. The water should be barely bubbling. If there was only enough water to cover half the chicken, then turn the chicken over and simmer for another 30 to 40 minutes. Otherwise, remove the chicken and allow to rest for a few minutes.

Using a pastry brush, coat the skin lightly with oil, if desired. Allow the chicken to rest for a further 20 to 30 minutes. When the chicken has cooled, carve or hack into bite-sized pieces with a sharp, heavy cleaver. Cut the green onion into round slices and sprinkle over the chicken. Garnish with cilantro. Serve with any of the dipping sauces under Toppings (see page 54).

You can use the soup right away for another purpose. If you bone the chicken prior to serving, or if you collect the bones at the end of the meal, you can boil them in the stock for another hour and thus have a very rich broth. During long banquets, this type of enriched broth simmered with cabbage and mushrooms is served at the end of the meal. This technique of "one dish, two ways" is used in simple country cooking—for example, with a fish—and it's also used in very sophisticated cooking, such as a Peking duck dinner, where the bones are later used to make a broth that comes at the end of the meal.

WOLFBERRY SOUP ᵛ

Wolfberry (Lycium sinense), whose Chinese name is gou qi zi, is a food so valued by the Chinese that emigrants have found a way to grow it wherever they have traveled in the world. It is rarely offered in restaurants because it is only available seasonally and it doesn't store well once picked. This has meant that the plant has remained a closely-guarded secret.

This dish combines the dried fruit with fresh leaves. Aside from being pleasant to eat—the fruit's hint of sourness and the grassy and astringent flavors of the leaves contrast well with rich broth—this soup is an excellent tonic for the eyes, liver, kidneys, and overall vitality.

The version presented here is simple and vegetarian. However, the soup can be made richer with the addition of shiitake mushrooms, tofu, bits of stewed meat or thin slices of pork liver.

The best fresh wolfberry plant is young, with the tips intact and unblemished. Older plants are just as good, but they have thorns along their stems. Stripping the leaves is easy: pull from the tip toward the base and you will never be hurt by the thorns.

Dried wolfberries are available in most Chinese supermarkets. They should be a bright orange-red in color.

You can use this same basic recipe for watercress, spinach, cabbage, or any leafy green plant. Trim the stems of 1 bunch of watercress or spinach, wash thoroughly, and plunge into boiling vegetarian or chicken stock. Serve as soon as the leaves turn a bright green. This simple soup is very healthful; in particular, watercress is good for the lungs. Combined with pieces of catfish, it makes an excellent soup for the convalescent. Spinach is a great source of iron and helps to build blood. Asian doctors prescribe this soup with slivers of red meat or liver.

Serves 4 to 6

4 ounces dried wolfberries
1 bunch wolfberry greens
6¼ cups Vegetarian or Chicken Stock (see pages 30 and 34)

Soak the dried fruit in water for a minimum of 20 minutes. Drain. Strip the wolfberry leaves from the stems and wash thoroughly.

Simmer the fruit in the stock until the fruit is plumped up. Turn up the heat. Add the leaves to the boiling broth. When the leaves turn a dark jade green, which will take a few minutes, remove from the heat and serve immediately.

THE LUNAR NEW YEAR

The Lunar New Year is a great time to begin your exploration of Zen cooking: it makes a perfect time to combine reverence and cuisine.

The date is different each year, so you'll have to consult local sources. Generally, however, the Lunar New Year falls on or about February 4th. If you live close to an Asian community, you'll see a big buildup of activity leading up to the actual day. Business people hurry to pay their debts and resolve accounts, and the markets will stock many foods traditional for the New Year. The quality will be very good.

All your shopping should be completed by the eve of the Lunar New Year. The day before New Year is the time to close the old year. Even if you aren't a vegetarian, you're supposed to be vegetarian on this day. Your house should be clean and your unfinished business resolved, and you should cook enough food to last at least through New Year's Day so you can present all your food before the gods.

Among the traditional dishes are Luohan vegetarian dishes, winter dumplings, minced oyster in lettuce cups, whole chickens, and whole fish (there's a great emphasis on wholeness in the foods). Tangerines and tangelos with leaves and branches still attached are part of the decor and the gifts you give to visiting relatives.

On New Year's Day, there should be no working, no cooking, no using knives, no arguing, and no scolding of children. Children, in fact, are to be completely indulged, and all children and unmarried members of the family receive "lucky money" in red envelopes from all married members of the family.

For Taoists and Buddhists alike, New Year is the time to set your sights on your spiritual goals, and to cook the dishes that symbolize your commitment. By being vegetarian during this period or the whole year, you show your desire for purity and gentleness. By presenting a whole fish and a whole chicken, you show your willingness both to begin and complete your tasks. To "have a head and a tail" is both a standard for a properly presented chicken or fish dish and a standard for completion in all your actions—surely the best of all New Year's resolutions.

WINTER SPHERES^v

This soup is a traditional dish served at New Year. The glutinous rice flour from which the dumplings are made is considered highly fortiifying by Taoist dietitians, so it makes both an economical and strengthening dish during the winter. The whiteness is a reminder of purity—the best of intentions should go into the coming year —and the round shape is a reminder of completeness, something to strive for in all endeavors.

The only constants in this recipe are the stock and the dumplings. Almost any other ingredient can be added. Common variations include nuts, cubed slices of any available vegetable, and slivers of meat.

You can also make a sweet version of this soup by bringing the stock to a simmer, then adding sugar until the broth is sweet to your taste. Add the dumplings and simmer over low heat for 20 minutes.

Serves 4

FOR THE DUMPLINGS
About 1 cup cold water
2 cups glutinous rice flour

FOR THE BROTH
4 cups Vegetarian or Chicken Stock *(see pages 30 and 34)*
4 ounces daikon (radish), cut into julienne
4 ounces napa cabbage or bok choy, cut into julienne
4 ounces carrots, cut into julienne
12 fresh shiitake mushrooms

To make the dumplings, slowly mix small amounts of cold water with the glutinous rice flour until a firm dough is formed. The amount of water will vary, so judge by the consistency of the dough. Knead until well mixed.

Dust a clean surface with rice flour and roll half of the dough at a time into a long cylinder about 1 inch in diameter. Cut into equal portions or simply pinch off enough to form into spheres about 1 inch in diameter. Place on a dish or baking sheet, cover with plastic wrap, and refrigerate overnight.

For the broth, bring the stock to a boil, then add all the other ingredients. Simmer the dumplings in the broth for 20 minutes. Serve.

RICE

Rice is at the center of many Asian meals. In Chinese communities, for example, rice is so much a part of eating that it is synonymous with dining itself. In China, rice was so precious that it came to symbolize happiness, nourishment, and fecundity. During imperial times, the emperor was responsible for many ceremonies, one of the most important being the sowing of rice. Rice reached Japan in the second century c.e., and became so important that feudal lords were ranked by the amount of rice their lands produced, and samurai were paid with rice. The deity Inari—the rice bearer—still has shrines throughout the Japanese countryside, and festivals surrounding the sowing, transplanting, and harvesting of rice are important parts of each year.

There are many types of rice, and the Zen cook would do well to experiment with as many of them as interest allows. To begin with, try long-grain white rice, which is delicious cooked so the grains are left relatively dry. Short-grain white rice—used almost exclusively in Japanese cooking—is much stickier and moister than long-grain. In Thailand, there is fragrant rice, or jasmine rice, which does indeed have a wonderful floral aroma. Sweet or glutinous rice is even more sticky than short-grain rice, and is famous as a source of energy. Finally, there are a number of colored rices, ranging from the familiar brown rice to red and black rice. In general, colored rice is an excellent source of fiber, and a great qi builder.

Rice has an inedible husk that must be removed. Beneath that is another layer, which contains many of the nutrients. This layer is left intact for brown rice, so using this as a staple can be a significant boon. Brown rice contains protein, fat, minerals, and a large amount of B vitamins, and it has fiber, which white rice lacks. Eating brown rice as a regular part of the diet can help lower cholesterol, reduce the risk of heart disease, improve digestion, and avoid cancers.

So rice, that essential ingredient, is actually a range of dishes that should be eaten according to the required role in the meal and the health needs of the people eating it.

PLAIN RICE ᵛ

When rice is being used as the basic staple of a meal, choose either long-grain or short-grain white or brown rice. Unprocessed rice is superior to processed or instant rice.

Many people, even traditionalists, have switched to electric rice cookers. These cookers help you determine the correct amount of water to add to the rice, and they automatically shift to a warming mode when the rice is done, thereby eliminating any possibility of the rice burning.

If you want to cook on the stovetop, use a heavy pot made of clay, glass, triple-clad stainless steel, or enameled cast iron. It is possible to use a thinner stainless steel pot, but the rice will have a tendency to burn at the bottom. Don't cook rice in bare cast iron.

Cooking rice is very simple, yet it vexes some people greatly. If you follow these steps, rice will become an easy staple for you to prepare any time.

Serves 4

2 cups rice
4 cups water

Measure your rice and put it into the pot. Wash thoroughly by pouring water over the rice and stirring with your hand. The water will turn cloudy. Pour off the water carefully, being mindful not to spill any grains of rice. Repeat until the water runs clear.

You can measure your water for rice, but those who cook rice frequently measure either by the knuckle method (touch the top of the rice with a finger and add water until the level comes up to the first knuckle—about 1 inch), or by tipping the pot (pour off excess water until the level of the water touching the rice is half the diameter of the pot).

If you are cooking on the stove top, add the water to the rice and bring to a boil. As soon as the water boils down so that it is just level with the surface of the rice, turn the heat down to its lowest setting

and cover the pot. Remove from the heat just when all the water has boiled away. In the beginning, you will have to uncover the pot to check. With practice, you will be able to sense this moment intuitively. Otherwise, don't uncover the pot of rice until it is done— so the qi of the rice will not escape. Allow the rice to sit with the cover on for a further 10 to 15 minutes after you have turned off the heat.

If you are using a rice cooker, place the rice in the cooker and follow the manufacturer's instructions. The cooker will automatically shut off at the proper time. Let the rice sit for 10 to 15 minutes after the bell has gone off.

Except in instances such as kaiseki cooking, stir or fluff the rice before serving. This helps to separate the grains and releases the fragrance of the rice.

THE RICE-POUNDER

When Buddha was once asked to preach to a gathering, he responded by raising a golden lotus, which had been offered to him. Of the many learned people there, only one, Mahakashyapa, smiled and nodded in understanding. That was the beginning of the special wordless transmission that is Zen.

Buddha lived in India. The twenty-eighth master, Bodhidharma, brought what is now called Zen to China. Five generations after Bodhidharma, a reputedly poorly-educated manual laborer from the south of China became the Sixth Master. Here is his story.

When it came time to select a successor, the aged Fifth Master announced that any monk who could prove his mastery of Zen would be given the symbols of authority over the entire sect: Bodhidharma's robe and begging bowl.

One of the learned disciples posted the following poem on the monastery wall:

This body is the Bodhi-tree
The soul is like the mirror bright:
Take heed to keep it always clean,
And let not dust collect upon it.

Everyone who read the poem was deeply impressed, and each was sure that the author would surely be named as the next master. But the next morning, they were surprised to see another poem posted beside the first, which said:

The Bodhi is not the tree
The mirror bright is nowhere shining:
As there is nothing from the first,
Where can the dust collect?

The author of this second poem, named Huineng, was a lowly rice-pounder who labored in the kitchen. Because of his humble status, the majority of monks were hostile to his audacious challenge. The Fifth Master, however, understood the rice-pounder's poem, and sent a secret message for Huineng to come at midnight. The master gave Huineng the robe and bowl.

PLAIN OR WHITE CONGEE^v

Congee is a thick rice porridge eaten at breakfast and as a late-night snack. By combining basic congee with various ingredients, some of which are medicinal herbs, congee can also be used as a means of adjusting one's health on a daily basis.

All Chinese medical doctors rely on the *Pen Cao*, the *materia medica* of Chinese herbal medicine. This book was first published in 1578 after twenty-six years of research by its author, Li Xizhen. Among its 1,892 entries, it features 8,162 prescriptions. On an equal footing with studies of the most rare of ginsengs is a long list of different congee. The inclusion of these recipes with formulas for healing serious disease is significant.

In the Chinese medical tradition, the heaviest emphasis is on preventative medicine. A doctor is considered good if he or she keeps patients healthy. In the wealthy homes of imperial China, a doctor was often employed to live in the household to keep all of its occupants from becoming ill. Similarly, temples usually had doctor-monks or doctor-nuns who supervised the diet. Congee became an essential food for the doctors to prescribe because it was plain and easily digested, and an ideal vehicle for herbs and foods.

Serves 4 to 6

1/4 cup long-grain rice
1/4 cup short-grain rice
8 cups water

Wash the rice according to the instructions given in the Plain Rice recipe (see page 39). Add the water. Bring to a boil, then reduce the heat as low as possible. Cover and simmer gently for 1 1/2 to 2 hours. Don't lift the lid during cooking, as it is believed this will allow the qi to escape. After cooking, the basic congee, called white congee, can be gently stirred with a paddle. Different ingredients can be added as toppings.
For a simple white congee, add a few slivers of freshly cut ginger to the porridge. Ginger neutralizes congee's cooling, yin nature. Other delicious toppings to add are:

Pickled ginger
Mustard Green Pickles (see page 45)
Roasted shelled peanuts
Green onions
Chiles in oil
Cilantro

White congee is considered an excellent meal for a person recovering from illness, and it is also eaten as a means of clearing the digestive tract. In some circles, for example, congee is eaten after a very rich meal in order to clean the body and bring it back to a more balanced level.

MUSHROOM AND CHICKEN CONGEE

This is an energy-giving dish. Chicken builds basic health, and mushrooms of all sorts not only provide essential minerals and fiber to the diet, but are also considered to help one to live longer. The most famous mushroom of all, the lingzi mushroom, is a first-class tonic and is extensively used to treat cancer patients. This recipe uses enoki mushrooms, but you should also try black mushrooms, which can be bought canned or dried (soak for several hours to rehydrate), fresh shiitake mushrooms, if they are available, or virtually any other kind of edible mushroom.

Serves 4

6 cups water
2 teaspoons soy sauce
2 teaspoons rice wine
2 chicken breasts
White Congee (see page 40)
2 ounces enoki mushrooms
4 green onions
1/2 cup roasted peanuts
6 slices fresh ginger, cut into slivers
Black sesame seeds

Bring the water to a boil, seasoning with the soy sauce and rice wine. Add the chicken breasts and simmer until barely cooked. (Test by poking with a chopstick to determine firmness; the firmer the meat, the more done it is.) Drain and allow to cool. Cut the chicken into slivers or hand-shred, discarding skin and bones.

Heat the congee in a saucepan. Wash the mushrooms and trim 1/2 inch from the base. Place in serving bowls, standing up against the side. Trim the roots from the green onions, and cut off all but about 3/4 inch of green. Split the onions lengthwise and place on either side of the mushrooms.

Spoon the hot congee into each bowl and distribute peanuts over the surface of the congee. Pile the chicken on top. Garnish with ginger and lightly sprinkle with black sesame seeds.

SWEET RED BEAN CONGEE[v]

This congee is a sweet soup. It is used to build blood and clear the digestion, and is a diuretic.

If you substitute Chinese green mung beans, which, like the red beans, are available dried, the character of the congee is changed to a cooling and thirst-quenching dish.

Serves 4 to 6

1/2 cup Chinese dried red beans
2 pieces zhen pei (*dried citrus skin*), or pared zest of 1 orange
4 cups water
White Congee (see page 40)
6 tablespoons sugar (*adjust to taste*)
2 teaspoons salt

Wash the red beans, discarding any broken beans or small rocks you might find. Combine the beans and zhen pei with the water in a saucepan. Bring to a boil, then cover and reduce the flame to its lowest. Simmer for 1 1/2 to 2 hours. Drain and discard the zhen pei.

Start the congee simmering in another pan; add the red beans and mix thoroughly. Cover and continue to simmer for at least another 30 minutes. Stir every 10 minutes or so and always cover the pot again. Add the sugar and salt in the last 10 minutes.

OTHER CONGEES

MEAT AND FISH CONGEES

Fish congee is easy to digest and is therefore often given to those who are convalescing. You can make it simply by placing boneless fish (perhaps marinated in soy sauce, rice wine, and sliced fresh ginger) in the bottom of a bowl and spooning boiling congee over it. By the time the congee is served, the fish will be cooked.

You can use the same method with most meats, as long as they are thinly sliced. A shortcut is to add the slivered meat to the congee itself and let the hot porridge do the cooking. Congee made with liver builds blood and is good for the eyes. Congee made with meat broth is used to build up very thin people. Frog is a congee favored by the wise.

LOTUS SEED CONGEEᵛ

This congee is a tonic for the spleen and stomach. Lotus seeds are available dried; simply wash a handful of the seeds and cook them with the congee.

CHESTNUT CONGEEᵛ

This congee builds up the kidneys and strengthens the legs. Use 32 chestnuts, either fresh or dried. If using fresh chestnuts, look for ones with firm shells (loose shells mean the chestnuts are not fresh). To remove the shells, score a deep X on the flat side of each nut using a chestnut knife, then simmer in water for about 10 minutes. Peel a few at a time, while they are still hot. (It's helpful to have several dish towels on hand to hold the chestnuts while you use your fingers or the chestnut knife to peel away the skins.) Peel away the furry inner skin, too. Bring a fresh pot of water to a boil and heat the chestnuts again; drain. Dried chestnuts, which are available in Chinese markets or supermarkets, need to be soaked for a few hours before cooking. Then simmer them in water for 30 minutes and drain.

Put the hot congee in bowls and top with the chestnuts. Alternatively, the chestnuts can be put into the water at the very beginning of cooking. The nuts will be much softer in texture and all the nutrients will go into the congee, but the flavors of the chestnut and congee will not be as distinct.

PINE NUT CONGEEᵛ

This congee moistens the heart and lungs and brings harmony to the large intestines. Toast 1 cup of pine nuts lightly in a nonstick frying pan. Blend in a food processor with enough stock to liquefy; the consistency should be like heavy cream. To serve, spoon the hot congee into serving bowls and pour a thin layer of the pine nut paste on top. Garnish with a few whole pine nuts.

This recipe can be adapted using either white or black sesame seeds instead of pine nuts.

VEGETABLE CONGEESᵛ

Other vegetables are used in congees as well. Taro congee is considered nutritious and helps very slim people to gain weight. Carrot congee relieves gas and promotes digestion. Celery congee is cooling in the summer and benefits the intestines. Leek congee warms the interior of the body. Wolfberry congee fortifies the blood and builds the kidneys. Fennel congee is beneficial to the stomach. Congee made with milk and honey is considered beneficial to the heart and lungs.

THE YELLOW MILLET DREAM

The Yellow Millet Dream was a Taoist parable that became a popular part of Chinese literature and drama. It features the meeting of two of the Eight Immortals, and summarizes the Taoist and Zen view of life as ephemeral.

Millet was eaten quite commonly in the past, but is not a part of the wider Asian diet today. It was cooked into a porridge similar to our congee recipes.

During the Tang dynasty, a weary young man named Lu Dongbin stopped at an inn. While the innkeeper began to cook millet, Lu fell into conversation with a Taoist priest who was also staying at the inn. Lu felt very comfortable speaking with Han Zhongli, the old Taoist, and eventually confessed his poverty. He voiced his desire to become a general or high official with great wealth and power. Seeing that the young man was so weary, the Taoist urged him to take a nap, and offered his own pillow. "Your wishes will all come true," Han Zhongli promised.

Lu dreamt that he married the beautiful daughter of a wealthy family, passed the imperial examinations, and was swiftly promoted. After taking command of a large army and driving back invaders, he rose to the office of prime minister. However, his rapid rise to power also brought jealousy and trouble to him, and he fell victim to court intrigues. His enemies accused him of organizing his border armies for a coup, and the emperor imprisoned Lu and his entire family.

Lu was so despondent that he was about to commit suicide when news came of his sentence: exile to a remote area. This he suffered through, until years later the emperor realized the mistake and restored him to the position of prime minister. He was given exactly the life that he had wished for in the inn: wealth, power, enormous land holdings, beautiful concubines, fine horses, and every luxury he could imagine. Again, however, there was a turn in his life. His wife became unfaithful, and he suffered many defeats in battle.

Lu Dongbin woke up. He was still in the inn, and the millet was still cooking. Han Zhongli smiled at him, and Lu experienced a great awakening.

MILLET ^v

Millet is quite nutritious, and its heartiness makes it suitable for people in cold climates. It is good for the stomach and spleen, and can take the place of rice in many meals. Millet posesses a wonderful range of textures: some grains will be soft as polenta, while others will be crunchy.

Serves 4 to 6

1 cup millet
3 cups water

Wash the millet, then drain as thoroughly as possible. Lightly dry-roast in a nonstick pan over medium heat. The aroma should be released quickly. Continue toasting for about 5 to 10 minutes. Keep the millet moving to avoid burning. Some of the grains will turn orange with the roasting.

Bring the water to a boil in a saucepan. Add the toasted millet. Cover, reduce heat, then simmer until all the water has been absorbed or boiled away—about 35 minutes.

MILLET CONGEE ^v

Serves 6 to 8

1 cup millet
1 teaspoon salt
6 cups water

Combine the millet, salt, and water in a pot and bring to a boil. Cover and simmer gently for 45 minutes. Serve in any of the same combinations given in the rice congee recipes.

MUSTARD GREEN PICKLES[v]

Pickles are an integral part of many Asian meals, and a featured part of temple cooking. With so many residents and visitors to feed, and with various crops to preserve, pickles are a natural option. Throughout most of Asian history, salt was difficult to obtain, and so having pickles was in some ways both a luxury and a health necessity. Today, however, excess salt is a danger, and so it's wise to limit the use of pickles or to lower the salt in other parts of the meal.

In traditional Chinese banquets, where each course serves both to delight the palate as well as contribute to a healthy progression of foods, pickles stimulate the digestive system as a part of the first course and prepare it for the rich foods to come.

Serves 8

8 ounces mustard greens, stems and leaf ribs only
1 cup granulated sugar
3 cups water
1 tablespoon salt
5 fluid ounces rice vinegar
4 slices fresh ginger

If you can, buy the young and tender "hearts" of mustard greens. Wash thoroughly, and cut into approximately 1-inch pieces.
Stir the sugar, water, salt, and vinegar in a saucepan over medium heat until the sugar is completely dissolved. Bring the mixture to a boil and simmer for 5 minutes. Remove from the heat and allow to cool.

Bring a large pot of water to a boil and blanch the mustard greens for 1 minute. Remove and cool immediately in cold water. Drain.

Place the mustard greens and ginger slices in a jar and fill with the sugar and vinegar mixture. The mustard greens must be completely covered. Cover the jar and refrigerate for 3 to 4 days before serving.

When ready to use, serve as is or chop into smaller pieces. Serve in 1-ounce portions as a seasoning for congee or plain rice, or chop very finely and cook on top of steamed meat. When using salted mustard green as a seasoning, reduce the amount of soy sauce or other salt added to the dish.

CUCUMBER AND CABBAGE PICKLES[v]

Pickling does not always have to take a long time. Sometimes, the pickling is done for only a few hours, resulting in pickles that are more akin to salads.

Some pickles are best prepared professionally. Traditionally, such pickles as the Takuan pickle in Japan, and many of the mustard green pickles in China, are bought from specialty merchants. Pickles exist in an enormous array in Asian markets, and you are encouraged to try them according to your palate.

Serves 6 to 8

3 small Japanese cucumbers, or ⅓ of an English cucumber
3 cabbage leaves
1 slice fresh ginger, shredded
1 tablespoon salt

Cut the cucumbers into round slices about ⅛ inch thick. Cut the cabbage into small, bite-sized pieces.

Combine all the ingredients in a bowl or glass dish, sprinkling thoroughly with salt. Put a piece of plastic wrap over the vegetables, followed by a dish and any weight like canned food, a clean brick, or a stone. Leave overnight.

Rinse before serving if you want to reduce some of the salt content.

CUCUMBER AND CABBAGE PICKLES WITH VINEGAR[v]

Serves 8 to 12

1 small head cabbage
1 cucumber
4 tablespoons salt
4 tablespoons rice vinegar

Pull the leaves from the cabbage, wash thoroughly, and cut into bite-sized pieces. Cut the cucumber into round slices about ⅛ inch thick. Combine all the ingredients in a jar or covered bowl and refrigerate for 3 to 5 days before serving.

THE VINEGAR-TASTERS

For those who would like a concise explanation of the differences between Confucianism, Buddhism, and Taoism, here is a perfect Zen-food story.

Confucius, Buddha, and Lao Zi gathered around a jar of vinegar. Each one dipped a finger in to taste it.

Confucius said that the vinegar was sour.

Buddha declared that the vinegar was bitter.

Lao Zi pronounced the vinegar sweet.

ASIAN LETTUCE SALAD

This salad is influenced by the flavors of China, Thailand, and Vietnam.

Serves 2 to 4

1 large head romaine lettuce
1/2 cup toasted pecans
2 teaspoons sugar
2 teaspoons toasted Sichuan peppercorns
1 tablespoon sesame seeds

FOR THE DRESSING
1 large egg yolk
1/2 cup olive or peanut oil
4 tablespoons walnut oil
4 tablespoons lime juice
2 teaspoons chile paste
2 large cloves garlic, very finely chopped
4 teaspoons fish sauce
1/2 teaspoon anchovy paste

Reserve the large outer leaves from the lettuce and tear the remaining lettuce into bite-size pieces.

Place the pecans in a heavy frying pan over medium heat and sprinkle with the sugar. Toss the pecans with the sugar until well coated and the sugar has melted to a caramel-like glaze. Set aside to cool.

Whisk the egg yolk in a bowl, then slowly add the olive and walnut oils 2 teaspoons at a time, whisking constantly. Add the lime juice, chile paste, garlic, fish sauce, and anchovy paste and whisk vigorously until the dressing is smooth.

Place the torn lettuce in a large bowl. Toss the lettuce with the dressing, then add the pecans and Sichuan peppercorns and toss again.

Place one large lettuce leaf on each plate and add the salad. Garnish with sesame seeds.

ASPARAGUS SALAD ᵛ

The contrast of flavors in this dish is striking: asparagus, pickled ginger, sesame oil, and chile all play major parts. As with all Zen cooking, the quality of each ingredient is of great importance.

Serves 4

8 ounces asparagus tips
2 teaspoons seeded and chopped tomato
Sesame seeds, to garnish

FOR THE DRESSING
2 tablespoons very finely chopped pickled ginger
1 fresh red jalapeño *(or any fresh hot red chile)*, or
1 tablespoon finely chopped red bell pepper
1 clove garlic, peeled
2 tablespoons rice vinegar
4 tablespoons olive oil
2 tablespoons pure sesame oil
2 teaspoons chopped sun-dried tomatoes packed in oil
1 tablespoon soy sauce
1 teaspoon balsamic vinegar
2 tablespoons chopped cilantro

Steam the asparagus for 3 to 5 minutes, until just tender but still bright green. The outer edges should be translucent, and the center should still be slightly opaque. Immediately place the asparagus into ice water until completely cooled, then drain.

Place the ingredients for the dressing in a blender or food processor and blend until smooth.

Sauce individual plates and arrange the asparagus spears on top. Garnish with the chopped tomatoes and a sprinkling of sesame seeds.

NOODLES

Noodles are widely available in such variety that you could eat a new dish every day for many months and not get tired of them. Noodles are easy to prepare and easy to digest. A bowl of hot noodles on a cold day is an undeniable comfort, and a bowl of cool noodles on a hot day is refreshing. If congee is the quintessential Zen breakfast, then noodles are the classic lunch and late-night snack food.

Many different noodles exist throughout Asia, and in each country they arouse great passion. China has three major types of noodles—wheat, rice, and bean. Wheat noodles are available in sizes ranging from very thin to a heavy, round noodle. Rice noodles are made in flat sheets that are then cut into various widths, from a thin, angel-hair style, to noodles as wide as a man's thumb. Bean noodles are made from soy, mung, and other beans. All noodles are available either fresh or dried, making them a very convenient food to have in your cupboard.

Vermicelli bean thread noodles, made from mung beans, are thin and white in color when you buy them. Dried white rice noodles (a wonderful ingredient in noodle dishes) look similar, so examine the package carefully. Incidentally, these noodles are often used as thickening agents in other dishes by being allowed to dissolve completely.

In Japan, there are buckwheat noodles called soba, and wheat noodles, which are either somen or udon. Soba noodles are considered so nutritious that some Buddhist ascetics lived on nothing but soba and fruit. One of the most common ways to serve soba is in a bowl with soup poured over them.

Other Asian countries also have famous noodles: both Vietnam and Singapore are known for their rice noodles. Korea has buckwheat noodles; the Philippines have pancit, a wheat noodle. There are so many variations that it's not surprising how popular noodles have become.

SOUP NOODLES WITH SLICED FISH

The many ways of serving noodles are as varied as their different forms. The following two recipes show a simple, nutritious, and basic method for preparing noodles in broth.

You can cook almost any type of vegetables and meat in soup this way. Popular vegetables include Chinese cabbages of all kinds, green beans, pea pods, cabbage, lettuce, soy and mung bean sprouts, and broccoli. Common meats include sliced beef, lamb, pork, chicken, and shrimp. In fact, it's possible to combine just about any foods and serve them on top of a mountain of steaming noodles in broth.

Serves 4

1 pound sliced rock cod or other white fish fillets
4 slices fresh ginger
3 fluid ounces rice wine
2 tablespoons soy sauce
1 pound fresh Chinese noodles or udon (*Japanese wheat noodles*)
4 cups Vegetarian or Chicken Stock (*see pages 30 and 34*)
8 ounces spinach
2 green onions, sliced
1 bunch cilantro

Cut the fish into slices against the grain. (Cutting from the inside of the fillet and at an angle toward the tail helps keep the pieces of fish from flaking apart during cooking.) Marinate for a minimum of 20 minutes in the ginger, wine, and soy sauce.

Bring a large stockpot of water to a boil. (There must be enough water to allow the noodles to separate and move freely.) Salting the water and adding a spoonful of oil are optional. When the water is boiling, add the noodles and pull them apart using long chopsticks or tongs. Cooking time will vary, depending on whether your noodles are fresh or dried, thin or thick: thin noodles should be cooked in as little as 10 seconds. Cook the noodles until they are soft, but not fully cooked. They should be slightly less than al dente.

Pour the noodles into a colander and rinse with cold water until the noodles are cool.

Bring the stock to a boil, and have the serving bowls close at hand. To heat the noodles, you can either put them all into the stock and then remove them with a long-handled strainer, or, if you are preparing one bowl at a time, you can put one serving of noodles into the strainer itself and then dip into the stock until the noodles are hot. After putting the noodles into serving bowls, spoon a little stock over them. Remember to undercook the noodles slightly as they will continue to cook in the bowls.

Plunge the spinach into the boiling broth. Remove with a strainer as soon as the leaves turn dark green—about 15 to 30 seconds. Using chopsticks or tongs, place a mound of spinach over the noodles in each bowl.

Cook the drained fish in the broth, either by adding all the slices at once, or by cooking in individual portions in the strainer. Cook until the fish is white and just cooked through but not falling apart. Arrange on top of the spinach. Strain more broth on top of each bowl, garnish with green onions and cilantro, and serve.

COLD SOBA NOODLES^v

Soba noodles are eaten either hot or cold. Hot noodles are prepared in a similar way to the following recipe. On hot days, cold noodles make a refreshing and nutritious alternative. More than one poet has rhapsodized about the pleasures of eating cool noodles on a sweltering day.

Again, there are many different ways of serving cold soba; this recipe is very simple. If you don't have seaweed, garnish with slivers of cucumber or pickled vegetables.

If you want to prepare this dish when the weather is very hot, serve the noodles in bowls of ice water. The sauce should be served separately for dipping, and other dishes and toppings served alongside the main dish.

Serves 4

1 pound dried soba *(Japanese buckwheat noodles)*
4 cups Basic Dashi *(see page 33)*
1 cup light soy sauce
1 cup mirin *(sweet rice wine)*
1 teaspoon powdered wasabi *(Japanese horseradish) (optional)*
4 pieces nori *(dried seaweed)*, cut into small strips
2 green onions, slivered

Fill a pot with enough water to allow all the soba to float freely. Bring to a boil. Add the soba. Using chopsticks or tongs, separate the noodles. Cook until barely soft, about 5 minutes. Drain the soba and chill in ice water. Drain again well.

Combine the dashi, soy sauce, mirin, and wasabi. Divide the noodles into bowls and pour the sauce over the noodles. Garnish with strips of seaweed and slivered green onions. Serve with other side dishes and toppings (see page 54).

VEGETARIAN SOUP NOODLES^v

The simple principle for making soup noodles is to combine a small portion of meat with a medium portion of vegetables and a large portion of noodles, all in a rich broth. In this vegetarian version, tofu provides the protein.

Straw mushrooms are available peeled or unpeeled. In their unpeeled form, the mushrooms are spherical; in their peeled form, they have a more normal mushroom profile. Straw mushrooms are occasionally available fresh, but are more commonly sold canned or dried. If you buy them canned, rinse the mushrooms well. If you buy them dried, rehydrate them before use by soaking in water until soft. Any other mushroom can be substituted.

Deep-fried tofu is available in stores, and you can use it in place of the fresh pressed tofu. The tofu can be paired with any number of leafy green vegetables, which can be quickly wilted in the broth and placed on top of the noodles before serving. Harder vegetables, such as turnips, lotus root and so on, should be parboiled first, as the carrots and broccoli are here.

Another way to add more flavor is to stir-fry the vegetables first, and then serve them on top of the soup noodles.

Pickles make a great topping, too, and seaweed shouldn't be overlooked either. When you're ready to serve, sprinkle slivered nori over the noodles.

Serves 4

1 pound fresh Chinese noodles or udon (*Japanese wheat noodles*)
4 cups Vegetarian or Chicken Stock (*see pages 30 and 34*)
1 slice fresh ginger
8 ounces broccoli florets
8 ounces carrots, cut into sticks
12 ounces pressed tofu, cut into 1/4-inch-thick slices
8 ounces canned straw mushrooms, peeled
Cilantro
2 green onions, cut into round slices

Cook the noodles as instructed in Soup Noodles with Sliced Fish (see page 49). Set aside after rinsing in cold water.

Put the stock and ginger in a large pot and bring to a boil. Add the broccoli and carrots in a wire basket. Remove when each is only about 80 percent cooked. Set aside.

Place the tofu and mushrooms in the wire basket and cook in the broth for about 3 minutes.

Divide the noodles into bowls. Arrange the broccoli, carrots, and straw mushrooms in small mounds on top. Add about 4 slices of tofu per person, fanning out the slices. Ladle hot broth on top, and garnish with cilantro and green onions.

TOPPINGS AND DIPPING SAUCES

Congees and soup noodles, as well as other recipes, are frequently served with a number of different toppings and dipping sauces. These are placed in small dishes, either individually before each diner, or in an eye-catching array to be shared by the whole table. Each guest can then add seasonings, flavors, and other nutritious foods to his or her bowl according to their taste or what they feel they need for their health. It's quite common for someone to say they feel that they need a certain food—say, something hot and spicy to counter damp weather. When different foods are available on the table, every diner can satisfy his or her palate and inner well-being without causing any offense to the chef or other guests or disturbing the gathering in any way.

The little dishes are very much like those presented before the altars in temples. Offering a variety of dishes symbolizes our wish to offer the entire world. In the same way, having a variety of dipping sauces and other condiments allows us to present a world of flavors to our guests.

WHOLE TOPPINGS

Unless the cook has already used some of these as garnishes, the following common toppings make delicious additions: cilantro, pickles, chiles, fresh basil, mung bean sprouts (some prefer to remove the yellow heads for a more refined presentation), roasted nuts (such as peanuts, almonds, cashews), slivered fresh ginger, very finely chopped garlic, seaweed, yellow chives, wedges of lemon or lime (juice is squeezed onto the dish), and sesame seeds.

SAUCES MADE AT THE TABLE^v

Dipping sauces can be used as condiments at the table, or they can be spooned over the noodles or other foods you have. Soy sauce, vinegar, chile oil, and oyster sauce (or its vegetarian equivalent, mushroom sauce) are basic sauces in bottles. At some tables, the basic bottles and ingredients are put out and each diner mixes his or her own based on the following proportions:

SOY AND CHILE DIP:
4 parts soy sauce and 2 parts chile sauce

SOY AND GARLIC DIP:
4 tablespoons soy sauce and 2 cloves garlic, very finely chopped

TOMATO, SOY, AND CHILE DIP:
4 parts tomato purée,
4 parts soy sauce, and 1 part chile sauce

SOY AND SHERRY DIP:
1 part soy sauce and 1 part dry sherry

SOY AND MUSTARD DIP:
4 parts soy sauce and
2 parts prepared mustard

CHILE AND VINEGAR DIP:
4 parts vinegar, 1 part chile oil,
and 4 parts olive oil

SPICY DIPPING SAUCES

Thailand and Vietnam have given us a full spectrum of lushly flavored sauces. Here are two wonderful dipping sauces.

THAI CHILE DIP *(makes 4 tablespoons)*: Combine 6 to 8 Thai bird chiles, or 3 serrano chiles, finely sliced, 1 clove garlic, very finely chopped, 2 tablespoons fresh lime juice, 3 tablespoons high-quality fish sauce, and 1/2 teaspoon sugar in a glass or porcelain bowl. Let sit for 30 minutes before serving.

VIETNAMESE GINGER AND LIME DIP *(makes about 5 fluid ounces)*: Combine 2 cloves garlic, sliced, 2 Thai bird chiles (or any other kind of hot chile), and 2 tablespoons finely chopped fresh ginger in a mortar and grind into a paste. Transfer to a bowl and add 4 tablespoons high-quality fish sauce, 2 tablespoons fresh lime juice, including pulp, 3 tablespoons hot water, and 4 tablespoons sugar. Mix well.

SEASONED SALT AND PEPPER^v

A dish of seasoned salt and pepper is often on the table. To make, preheat a clean and dry nonstick frying pan. Add 2 teaspoons freshly ground black pepper and 2 tablespoons salt. Heat for 1 to 2 minutes, moving the mixture constantly. Serve in small dishes around the table so that each guest can dip a piece of food into the mixture according to his or her taste.

FAVA BEANS IN RED PEPPERS ᵛ

This recipe and the one that follows show two ways to prepare fresh beans just when they are at their peak. Fava beans are one of the pleasures of spring, and a wonderful sign that the warm season is approaching. These beans are available at other times of the year, dried, canned, or frozen, but they are best when young and fresh, just as they are coming into season. That is when their full beauty is revealed. Their flavor is so subtle, and their nutrients so valuable, that it is best not to overcook them.

If you are fortunate enough to get the youngest and most tender of beans, they may only need to be removed from their pods and you may not have to remove their skins. Otherwise, follow the procedure below.

The pale green beans make a wonderful contrast to the pepper cup in this recipe, but alternatively you can simply serve them in a dark bowl. This dish goes well with side dishes of pickles, rice, noodles, and other vegetables.

Makes 4 appetizer-sized portions

2 red peppers, cut in half crosswise and seeds removed
2 cups shelled fresh fava beans

FOR THE BROTH
6¼ cups water
4 tablespoons sake
4 teaspoons sugar
2 teaspoons soy sauce
1 teaspoon salt

Place the broth ingredients in a saucepan and bring to a boil.

Trim the base of each bell pepper half so that it forms a cylinder that will sit well on a plate. Plunge the bell pepper halves into the broth, and simmer with the lid off until soft—about 2 minutes. Remove and place in cold water. When the bell peppers are cool, take from the water and drain. Set aside.

Put the fava beans into the simmering broth and cook for 1 to 2 minutes. Remove from the broth with a long-handled strainer and put into a bowl of cool water. Slip the tender beans from the tough skins, if necessary.

Return the fava beans to the simmering broth and cook for a further 4 minutes or until tender. Drain. Save the broth for another use, or store to add to stock.

Arrange the beans in the bell pepper cups or in a bowl. Serve either hot or at room temperature.

SPINACH SALAD WITH GRILLED TOFU^v

One great virtue of tofu is its ability to absorb flavors from other foods or seasonings. Marinating and grilling give tofu a particularly rich flavor, especially
good for tempting those who are used to meat as the center of a dish. In
China, tofu is marinated in a variety of ways, but the technique of grilling it
is a recent Western innovation. This salad uses tofu in a way that is easy to
prepare and sure to appeal to many different palates.

Serves 4

1 pound firm tofu
2 teaspoons olive oil
4 ounces fresh shiitake mushrooms, stems removed and thinly sliced
8 ounces spinach leaves, washed *(weighed after trimming)*
1/2 medium purple or red onion, thinly sliced
2 tablespoons toasted sunflower seeds
1 tablespoon toasted sesame seeds

FOR THE MARINADE	FOR THE DRESSING
4 tablespoons balsamic vinegar	**1/2 teaspoon Dijon mustard**
2 teaspoons soft brown sugar	**2 to 3 cloves garlic, very finely chopped**
2tablespoons olive oil	**1 tablespoon fermented black beans,**
2 teaspoons sesame oil	**rinsed and drained**
1/2 cup rice wine	**1 teaspoon chile paste**
1/2 cup soy sauce	**1 teaspoon grated fresh ginger**
1/4 teaspoon five-spice powder	**4 tablespoons olive oil**
1 tablespoon chipotle or other hot	**1 tablespoon balsamic vinegar**
chile powder *(optional)*	**1 tablespoon soy sauce**
	2 tablespoons orange juice

Cut the tofu into 1-inch cubes. Combine the ingredients for the marinade in a bowl and add the tofu. Marinate for at least 4 hours or
overnight in the refrigerator. Whisk together the dressing ingredients.

Heat the 2 teaspoons olive oil in a large nonstick frying pan (use
4 teaspoons oil in a wok or other pan) over medium heat. Add the
tofu when the oil is hot and gently fry until crisp on all sides (about
15 minutes). Remove from the pan and set aside.

Lightly sauté the sliced mushrooms with 2 tablespoons of the dressing until just softened, with edges slightly translucent. Remove from
the heat.

Blanch the spinach briefly in a pot of boiling water; remove when
the spinach is just barely wilted. Drain well. Toss with 2 tablespoons
of the dressing. Arrange the mushrooms on top of the spinach.

Toss the onion and tofu with the remainder of the dressing and
arrange over the mushrooms and spinach. Garnish with toasted sunflower and sesame seeds.

SOYBEAN SPROUT SOUP ᵛ

Soy protein is an important part of Zen cooking. If you are a vegetarian, it is one of the cornerstones of building a diet with enough protein. Even if you aren't a vegetarian, soy protein is valuable. There is ample evidence that a diet with adequate soy protein can help fight heart disease and cancer.

Soybean sprouts are used in soups, salads, and stir-fries. The beans themselves are consumed whole, or ground into various soy milks, noodles, and cakes, or preserved in sheets and sticks, or made into soy sauce. Various forms of soy are even sweetened for pastries.

Soybean sprouts are nutritious, and make a wonderful addition to any dish because they can take a great deal of cooking and still retain their texture. A soy sprout soup is richly nutritious and easily digested, leaving your system clear and invigorated.

Serves 4

About 2 cups loosely packed soybean sprouts
6¼ cups Vegetarian or Chicken Stock (see pages 30 and 34)
8 fresh shiitake mushrooms or soaked dried black mushrooms
2 ounces firm tofu, cut into ½-inch cubes
Salt to taste
1 green onion, cut into thin rounds
4 tablespoons alfalfa sprouts

Place the soy sprouts in a sieve and pour boiling water over them to remove any mustiness left from the sprouting process.

Bring the stock to a boil. Add the whole mushrooms and soy sprouts and simmer for 20 to 30 minutes. This soup is very forgiving as far as cooking time—some cooks simmer this soup much longer over a low fire.

Add the tofu for the last 10 minutes of cooking. Season with salt to taste. Garnish with a sprinkling of green onion and alfalfa sprouts before serving.

SOYBEANS IN PODS ᵛ

In the autumn, fresh soybeans in the pod are a signal that it's harvest time. It is then that the beans are available, already prepared, in Japanese markets, labeled as edamame. You don't have to do anything but bring them home, cook, and serve them. Each guest will squeeze the pod and the green soybeans will come out easily. Like fava beans, soybeans are always available dried, but they are a very special seasonal treat when eaten fresh.

Makes 4 appetizer-sized portions

12 ounces fresh young soybeans in pod
Salt

Wash the soybean pods.

Salt a saucepan full of water to taste and then bring to a boil. Add the soybeans and cook until tender, about 5 minutes. Drain and cool. Serve in small dishes with sake, beer, or tea. Each guest can remove his or her own beans from the pods. Alternatively, you can remove the beans for them and serve like the fava bean recipe on page 56.

The soybeans can also be removed from their pods and then used as toppings for salads, congees, or noodles.

TOFU STICKS AND LAMB STEW

Tofu sticks packaged in dry form are available in Chinese markets. Yellowy-beige in color, they are a thin sheet of bean curd rolled into a stick form and then dried. This recipe is derived from classic northern Chinese cuisine and is a cold-weather dish. The Taoists regard lamb as a tonic to the blood and fortifying to the body.

Serves 4

1 pound boneless lamb stew meat, cut into chunks
2 tablespoons soy sauce
2 tablespoons rice wine
6 cloves garlic, smashed
2 ounces *(dry weight)* **tofu sticks**
6 ounces carrots, peeled
2 tablespoons canola oil
3 cups Chicken Stock *(see page 34)*
1 thumb-size piece fresh ginger, sliced
1 bay leaf
8 ounces canned unpeeled straw mushrooms
3 tablespoons cornstarch *(optional)*
Freshly ground pepper to taste
Cilantro to garnish

Marinate the lamb with the soy sauce, wine, and garlic for a minimum of 30 minutes. Soak the tofu sticks in water until soft, then cut into roughly 2-inch sections. Cut the carrots using a swivel cut (turn carrot with every cut so all pieces are angular and irregular).

In a pot, sear the lamb in the hot oil, then add the stock, ginger, and bay leaf. Bring to a boil. Cover, reduce to a simmer, and cook for at least 1 1/2 hours, skimming off fat occasionally.

Add the tofu sticks, mushrooms, and carrots and cover the pot again. Cook for a further 30 minutes. If you want a thicker sauce, mix the cornstarch with a little water and add a little at a time, stirring. Season with freshly ground pepper. Remove from the heat.

Put a generous amount of cilantro on top of the stew, and cover briefly until the cilantro has wilted. Serve.

SLIVERED TOFU AND CELERY ˅

Pressed and marinated tofu is available fresh, often vacuum sealed, in the refrigerated section of the market. It is a block or cake of tofu that has had much of the liquid pressed out of it, leaving a dense cake about 1/4-inch thick. These cakes, which have a somewhat cheese-like texture, are available both plain and already marinated in soy and five-spice mixtures. The following recipe uses soy-marinated tofu.

If you like, you can make your own pressed tofu by putting a cake of firm tofu on a board, covering it with cheesecloth, muslin, or plastic wrap, and then pressing it down with something flat and about 2 1/2 pounds in weight. Leave it for at least 1 hour until all the liquid has been pressed out. Pat dry. The resulting cake can be used as is, or marinated like meat.

Serves 4

8 ounces celery
6 ounces pressed soy-marinated tofu
4 ounces fresh bamboo shoot *(or, if canned, buy whole shoots)*
3 ounces soaked dried or canned black mushrooms
1 small red bell pepper
1 teaspoon canola oil
4 slices fresh ginger
1 green onion, slivered, to garnish

Cut the celery, tofu, bamboo shoot, mushrooms, and bell pepper into pieces about 1/4 inch thick and 2 inches long. Heat a nonstick pan over high heat and add the oil (increase amount of oil if using an uncoated pan). Begin stir-frying the celery first. Then add the tofu, bamboo shoot, and ginger after about 30 seconds. After a further 2 minutes, add the black mushrooms and bell pepper. Turn constantly, but be careful not to break up the tofu. Remove the vegetables when they are hot and when the celery is translucent, but before the bell pepper has lost its vivid color. Garnish with slivers of green onion and serve.

IMPERIAL TOFU

The history of tofu is controversial. One story is that a baron named Liu An invented bean curd during the Han dynasty (206 b.c.e–220 c.e.). Like the First Emperor of China, Liu had an extraordinary interest in creating the Taoist elixir of immortality, and is said to have invented tofu during his experiments. Because bean curd is easy to digest, people tend to eat more of it as they age, and so it has come to be known as a food of longevity, even if it isn't literally the elixir of immortality.

Tofu is usually made by special bean-curd makers. The mills for bean curd are large, and many sacks of beans are soaked and then ground each morning. Tofu is made by straining the resulting slurry and then coagulating it with a substance like gypsum to precipitate the proteins. The resulting mass is strained again before being pressed into cakes.

Soy milk, one of the products also produced by the bean-curd makers, is served warm as a breakfast drink in Asia. People think of drinking warm soy milk in the morning with the same emotion as others might over the aroma of good coffee. In order to supply the soy milk so early in the morning, the bean-curd makers must work very hard during the night. A folk saying notes that being a bean-curd maker is one of the most difficult of fates.

Tofu is readily available, and it is eaten by most people in Asia, regardless of class. It makes an excellent substitute for meat, even for those who are near-vegetarian because of the poverty of their circumstances rather than their philosophy or beliefs.

GRILLED MUSHROOM, TOFU, AND EGGPLANT LAYERS^V

This recipe uses four kinds of mushrooms— portobello, shiitake or black, oyster, and enoki.

When you buy dried black mushrooms, look for mushrooms of similar diameter throughout the package. Although the mushrooms are dry, they should not be withered, nor should they have any bad spots on them. After rehydrating them by soaking them in water for at least 2 hours or overnight, most people break off the stems, which can be kept for making stock. There are many forms of dried mushrooms, both from China and Japan, and there is a considerable range in price from fairly reasonable to incredibly expensive. Like so many things, the higher the cost, the better the quality and flavor tend to be.

Serves 4

1¼ pounds firm tofu, divided into 4 cakes
Canola oil
4 portobello or large open cap mushrooms, each about 3 inches in diameter
4 large slices of eggplant each about ½ inch thick and 3 in inches diameter
4 ounces fresh shiitake mushrooms or soaked dried or canned black mushrooms
4 ounces oyster mushrooms
1 cup Vegetarian Stock (see page 30)
½ cup mushroom or oyster sauce
4 tablespoons rice wine
6 slices fresh ginger, slivered
3 ounces enoki mushrooms
2 green onions chopped

Press the tofu (see page 60); or buy already-pressed tofu. Pat each pressed cake dry with a towel, then rub with oil.

Rub the portobello mushrooms and eggplant with oil. Grill the mushrooms, eggplant, and tofu cakes, turning once, over a charcoal fire, or on a heated ridged cast-iron grill pan, until the mushrooms and eggplant are well marked and soft and the tofu is marked and golden on both sides. When done, place a tofu cake on each plate, put on an eggplant slice, and top with a portobello mushroom. Keep warm.

Put 1 tablespoon oil in a nonstick pan (use about 3 tablespoons oil if cooking in an uncoated pan) and bring to a high heat. Rapidly stir-fry the shiitake and oyster mushrooms, being careful not to break up or burn the mushrooms. Cook until the mushrooms are half-soft and the edges are slightly seared— about 3 minutes.

Add the stock, mushroom sauce, rice wine, and ginger and stir over high heat for 2 minutes. Add the enoki mushrooms and green onions last, cooking for about 1 minute. Pour this sauce over the grilled portobello, eggplant, and tofu layers. Serve with rice.

PURE STIR-FRY [v]

An important basic dish to master is stir-fried vegetables. The Chinese cabbage, bai cai, or bok choy as it is called in Cantonese, is fast becoming popular in many markets, and is an essential vegetable in Asian cooking. It is available nearly all year-round, and is an excellent source of calcium, iron, and fiber. Like all vegetables, it is cooling to the system, but stir-frying and the addition of a little ginger renders it more neutral and harmonious. A simple meal of rice and stir-fried vegetables can be very satisfying.

There is a mode of cooking that translates as "pure stir-fry," or "clear cooking." When you use this term, you mean vegetables cooked without a great deal of added flavor. With high-quality ingredients, the natural flavors of the ingredients will be foremost.

This means that you need to have perfect Chinese cabbage. Some bok choy piled up at markets is so fresh that it seems almost iridescent. The best bok choy are bok choy hearts, also called baby bok choy. Although bok choy can grow to lengths of 12 inches or more, the most tender and delicious are younger ones measuring 4 to 6 inches in length. These should have thick green leaves without yellow spots or insect damage. The stems are best when they are a smooth pale green, unblemished and firm to the touch. When you look at the base of the vegetable, the cut should be moist, with no cracks through the heart.

You can use clear stir-frying for virtually any vegetable—spinach, watercress, lettuce, cabbage, chard, and the delicious pea sprouts. Vegetables such as zucchini and other summer squash, peppers, and so on need to be sliced or diced before stir-frying. Harder vegetables, such as broccoli and cauliflower, must be blanched first (see Five-Color Stir-fry on page 66).

Stir-frying with any meat is based on simple principles. Slice the meat thinly. Marinate it, if you like. Stir-fry the meat over high heat until it is half-cooked, then remove it. Cook whatever vegetables you'd like until they are nearly done, then add the meat back in, stir-fry briefly, add stock, and thicken the gravy before serving.

If you remember these simple principles, then you can also use mushrooms or tofu in the same role as the meat. Stir-fry them first so you can control the degree of cooking they might need, and so you can use them to flavor the pan before adding the vegetables.

Serves 4

1 pound bok choy hearts
1 teaspoon peanut or canola oil
2 slices fresh ginger
2 cloves garlic, smashed
2 teaspoons light soy sauce
2 teaspoons rice wine
1 teaspoon sugar (optional)
½ cup Vegetarian Stock (see page 30)

Wash the bok choy thoroughly. Break off the stem, and trim the base slightly. Check each stem for dirt, and wash well.

Heat a nonstick pan to medium-high heat.

Add the oil. (If you are using an iron pan or wok, make sure it is well-seasoned and use only enough oil to coat the pan.) Add the slices of ginger and the garlic, which will neutralize any iron taste from the pan and enhance the flavor of the dish. Add the bok choy, both leaves and stems, to the pan just before the oil begins to smoke. There should be a loud sizzling sound that will continue throughout the cooking. If there isn't enough sound, your pan needs to be hotter. Add the soy sauce, wine, and sugar if desired.

Turn the bok choy rapidly with a spatula. The pan should be hot enough that the vegetables seem to cook nearly instantly. You should hear your cooking, and smell the ginger, vegetables, oil, and wine. After a few seconds, add the stock.

The bok choy should be removed when not quite fully cooked, for it will continue to cook on the way to the table. You want it to be completely done just as it is eaten: It should be cooked, hot, and yet still a little crunchy. When you bite into the stems, they should release a great deal of juice. In order to gauge this correctly, look at the vegetables. The leaves should be a deep dark green, in fact more vibrant and darker than before they were cooked. The stems should just be turning translucent, like the color of fine, pale jade. That is the moment you should remove the ginger and garlic, arrange the vegetables in a simple heap, and bring them quickly to the table.

FIVE-COLOR STIR-FRY ˅

Once you master the pure or clear stir-fry technique, you can adapt it to virtually any vegetable. This dish takes the basic stir-fry technique and applies it to the Taoist theory of the five elements.

The Taoists describe all things as coming from five elements—water, wood, fire, earth and metal. Rather than view these as literal elements, it is best to think of each of them in terms of their archetypal nature. For example, water is cooling, and flows and moves downward; fire is hot and expansive. Over thousands of years, the five elements have been used as the theoretical basis for everything from martial arts to medicine, and from cosmology to folk art.

Since the five elements represent everything in the universe, and since the best aspects of health reflect balance both inside and outside the body, it is natural to use the five elements as part of your diet, too. There is an easy way to do that, because each of the five elements is associated with a color. If you make a dish of vegetables using each of the five colors, then you will have a meal that is inherently balanced. Put that dish together with rice, noodles, or bread, and you will have a most satisfying and healthy meal.

The five colors are black, green, red, yellow, and white. In this dish, mushrooms, broccoli, carrots, bamboo shoots, and water chestnuts represent the five colors. Once you have learned this way of combining foods, the variations are endless.

Serves 4

4 ounces broccoli florets
4 ounces cauliflower florets
4 ounces carrots, cut into 1-inch pieces
1 teaspoon peanut or canola oil
2 slices fresh ginger
2 cloves garlic, smashed
4 ounces fresh shiitake mushrooms or soaked dried black mushrooms
4 ounces fresh bamboo shoots or whole canned bamboo shoots, sliced
2 teaspoons light soy sauce
2 teaspoons rice wine
1 teaspoon sugar *(optional)*
1/2 cup Vegetarian Stock *(see page 30)*
2 tablespoons cornstarch

Blanch the broccoli, cauliflower, and carrots in boiling water until barely softened. Drain.

Heat a nonstick pan on medium-high heat, then add the oil. (If you are using a well-seasoned iron pan or wok, use enough oil to coat the pan.) Add the ginger and garlic. Stir-fry the mushrooms first, and remove when they are nearly cooked. Set them aside. Stir-fry the broccoli, cauliflower, and carrots next, tossing gently until they are seared but not broken up. Then add the bamboo shoots. Finally,

return the mushrooms to the pan. Add the soy sauce, wine, and sugar. When the vegetables are almost cooked, or if the pan becomes dry, add the stock.

If you want a thicker sauce, push the vegetables to the sides of the pan when they are about 80 percent cooked, creating a "well" for the sauce in the center. Mix the cornstarch with a little water and slowly add to the pan, stirring constantly, until the sauce is as thick as you like. Turn the vegetables in the sauce a few more times, and serve.

LUOHAN VEGETABLE STEW^v

The many versions of Luohan Zhai—luohan is a Buddhist saint and zhai means a vegetarian dish—were all inspired by the cooking at Buddhist temples. In fact, Buddhists and those interested in spiritual matters are often called "zhai-eaters." Traditionally, a Lunar New Year's celebration always includes the eating of zhai.

Zhai usually features a combination of fresh and dried vegetables. When dried, vegetables have different, often stronger flavors than when they are fresh.

Serves 4 to 6

2 ounces *(dry weight)* tofu sticks
1/2 ounce *(dry weight)* lily bud stems
1/4 ounce *(dry weight)* black tree ears
8 fresh shiitake mushrooms or dried black mushrooms
3 ounces fresh or canned ginkgo nuts
3 ounces fresh water chestnuts
3 ounces pea pods
5 1/2 ounces vermicelli bean thread noodles
1 tablespoon canola oil
4 slices fresh ginger
4 cloves garlic, smashed
3 ounces carrots, cut into julienne
4 cups Vegetarian Stock *(see page 30)*
1 tablespoon soy sauce
1 teaspoon hoisin sauce
2 tablespoons rice wine
1 teaspoon sugar
2 teaspoons cornstarch mixed with a little water or stock
2 tablespoons pure sesame oil
2 green onions
Cilantro to garnish

Soak all the dried ingredients—the tofu sticks, lily bud stems, tree ears, and whole black mushrooms—in water to cover for at least 1 hour or until they are soft. Drain. The water from the black mushrooms can be added to the stock.

Shell the ginkgo nuts. Prepare the water chestnuts by cutting the base off with a sharp knife and then, using a vegetable peeler, peeling off the brown skin to reveal the white inside. Pea pods should have the "string" pulled off: Break off each end and pull toward the opposite end of the pod.

Prepare the vermicelli bean thread noodles by placing them in a strainer and pouring boiling water over them. Set aside.

Heat a large nonstick pan and add the oil. Sauté the ginger and garlic together briefly. Add the carrots, tofu sticks, lily bud stems, tree ears, and shiitake or black mushrooms and stir-fry for 5 minutes.

Pour 3 cups of the stock over the ingredients in the pan. Stir in the soy and hoisin sauces, rice wine, and sugar. When the liquid is well mixed, add the vermicelli noodles. Separate them with chopsticks, and distribute them evenly throughout the dish. Cover the pan, turn the flame down so the liquid is just boiling, and simmer for about 5 minutes.

Add the ginkgo nuts, pea pods, and water chestnuts. Add the remainder of the stock. Cook for a further 3 to 5 minutes.

Turn up the flame. Thicken the sauce with the cornstarch mixture, if desired. Add the sesame oil. Mix thoroughly, then serve, garnished with green onions and cilantro.

SOME INGREDIENTS THAT MAY SOUND UNFAMILIAR

Ginkgo Nuts *These may be bought loose or canned, but the fresh ones, generally available in the autumn and winter, are best. Ginkgo nuts are believed to be cooling and detoxifying, and are excellent for the system. Their slightly bitter taste is more than compensated for by the wonderful texture of the nut itself. Turkey, traditionally eaten on the American holiday of Thanksgiving, is thought to be overly taxing to the system. Since the time of year coincides with the ginkgo nut season, many stores in American Chinatowns put up signs saying "Eat fresh ginkgo nuts after Thanksgiving."*

Fresh nuts come in smooth, hard white shells. Avoid any punctured or broken shells, since the nut will probably be moldy. Each nut must be shelled. Hold the nut with its most pointed side down and hit the other end with a hammer. Remove the nut from the shell. If there is a brown skin on the nut, soak briefly in water to help loosen and remove it.

Black Tree Ears *This is a fungus that grows on trees, hence the name. While the idea of eating fungus may put some people off, remember that mushrooms are also fungi. Black tree ears recently became very popular when Western studies showed that eating them lowered blood pressure.*

Look for the smallest ones. If you do buy the larger sizes, they will require longer soaking and cutting into slivers.

Lily Bud Stems *The Chinese name for these translates as "golden needles." These are bought dried and should be soaked before use.*

MINCED CHICKEN WITH PRAWNS

Dishes that combine chicken and prawns are called "Dragon and Phoenix." Yang is the Taoist term for any force or thing that is male, positive, light, and hot. Yin is the term for anything female, nega- tive, dark, and cold. Thus, to have dragon and phoenix is to have yang and yin, and to have a dish that symbolizes cosmic whole- ness. This dish uses some of the most popular Southeast Asian spices.

Serves 4 to 6

1 whole chicken breast, boned, skinned, and minced
5 tablespoons rice wine
1/2 teaspoon salt
4 tablespoons cornstarch
1 pound raw shrimp or prawns, shelled and deveined
5 slices fresh ginger, 3 of them left whole and 2 very finely chopped
2 teaspoons canola oil
2 tablespoons very finely chopped shallots
3 cloves garlic, very finely chopped
2 fresh hot red or green chiles, very finely chopped, or
3 tablespoons very finely chopped red or green bell pepper
2 teaspoons soy sauce
1 cup Chicken Stock (see page 34)
1 bunch fresh basil leaves, cut into thin strips
2 green onions, finely chopped

Mix the minced chicken with 2 tablespoons of the rice wine, the salt and 1 tablespoon of the cornstarch. Marinate for 10 to 30 minutes.

At the same time, marinate the shrimp with 2 tablespoons of the rice wine, the 3 slices of ginger, and 1 tablespoon cornstarch for 10 to 30 minutes. Mix the remaining cornstarch with a little water and set aside.

Put 1 teaspoon of the oil in a nonstick pan (or use 4 tablespoons oil in a wok or frying pan) and bring to a high heat. Add the chicken mixture and stir-fry until it just turns white and the pieces become sep- arate. The chicken should only be about two-thirds cooked. Remove the chicken to a strainer or paper to drain.

Clean the pan, then heat the remaining 1 teaspoon oil over medium heat (or use the remaining oil in a wok or other pan). Cook the shallots until they are just translucent. Add the chopped ginger and garlic and stir-fry for about 30 seconds. Add the shrimp and continue to stir-fry. Add the chiles. When the shrimp begin to curl and turn pink, add the soy sauce and remaining 1 tablespoon rice wine.

Return the chicken to the pan. Add the stock. Turn the heat to high, then add the basil. Make a "well" in the center of the pan by pushing the ingredients away. Slowly add the cornstarch mixture to the pan, stirring, until the sauce thickens to your preference and the basil is wilted. Stir the entire dish thoroughly. Remove from the heat, garnish with chopped green onions, and serve with rice.

PACIFIC RIM ENCHILADAS

Food wrapped in flat bread is popular the world over. From the steppes of Mongolia to the jungles of Yucatan, from the ubiquitous mu shu pork of Chinese restaurants to the burritos from street vendors in Mexico, there are hundreds of different ways to wrap food. Here is a dish that takes its inspiration from the Mexican enchilada, but uses ingredients from around the Pacific Rim—shiitake mushrooms from Japan, water chestnuts from China, lime and coconut from Thailand, tomato from the Americas.

You use flour tortillas, which should be as fresh as possible and at room temperature.

Serves 4

1/2 cup Chicken Stock (*see page 34*)
8 sun-dried tomato halves (*not packed in oil*)
2 chicken breast fillets, sliced into thin
2-inch strips
1 teaspoon hot chile powder or paprika
1 teaspoon ground cumin
1 teaspoon ground coriander
1 teaspoon white pepper
Pinch of salt
1 tablespoon dry sherry
1 tablespoon lime juice
1 egg white, slightly beaten
2 teaspoons cornstarch
1 tablespoon canola oil
1 tablespoon very finely chopped fresh ginger
2 cloves garlic, very finely chopped
1 cup fresh shiitake mushrooms, thinly sliced

1/2 cup coconut milk
4 to 6 fresh water chestnuts, peeled and sliced
4 green onions, very finely chopped
1/2 cup cilantro, finely chopped
Toasted sesame seeds to garnish

FOR THE SAUCE
2 tablespoons olive oil
1 large onion, very finely chopped
1 teaspoon ground allspice
3 cloves garlic, very finely chopped
1 red bell pepper, roasted, peeled, and coarsely chopped
2 1/2 cups Chicken Stock (*see page 34*)
1/2 cup coconut milk
1 teaspoon soy sauce,
1 tablespoon toasted sesame seeds
2 teaspoons lime juice

In a small saucepan, bring 1/2 cup of the chicken stock to a boil, then remove from the heat. Place the sun-dried tomatoes in the stock and cover. Leave to soak for 20 to 30 minutes to rehydrate. Remove the tomatoes from the stock, squeezing out excess liquid, and finely chop. Set the tomatoes and tomato stock aside.

To make the sauce, heat the olive oil over medium-high heat in a heavy medium-sized saucepan. Add the onion and sauté until very dark golden brown. This is a caramelizing process and should take 8 to 10 minutes. Add the allspice and garlic and stir, then

add the roasted bell pepper, chicken stock, coconut milk, and soy sauce. Simmer over medium heat for 20 minutes. Remove from heat. Add the sesame seeds and lime juice and stir. Purée in a blender, in small batches, until very smooth. Return to the saucepan and leave to reheat at a low simmer while preparing the filling.

Toss the chicken with the chile powder, cumin, coriander, pepper, and salt. Then toss with the lime juice and sherry. Add the egg white and mix together thoroughly. Add the cornstarch and coat the mixture well. Set aside.

Heat the oil in a wok or large frying pan over high heat until just smoking. Add the ginger and then the chicken mixture and toss vigorously, cooking until the pieces become separate. Add the garlic and continue stir-frying. Add the mushrooms and toss with the chicken for about 1 minute, then add the coconut milk, tomato stock, and remaining chicken stock. Cook until the sauce thickens and clings to the chicken and mushrooms. Add the water chestnuts, green onions, and cilantro. Cook for about 1 minute longer, making sure all the ingredients are thoroughly mixed together. Reduce the heat to very low to keep the filling warm.

Working quickly, roll about 1 1/2 tablespoons of the chicken filling into each tortilla. Divide among 4 plates. Generously ladle the sauce. Garnish with toasted sesame seeds and serve.

ASIAN JAMBALAYA

This is a perfect dish to make if you are serving a larger group of people. Although you may have to make a special trip to a Chinese market for the sausage, you will find it well worth your time. Be sure the sausage is lean. Remember to buy fresh mussels and test by checking that they retract when poked, and have a sweet, seasalt smell. Dead shellfish deteriorate quickly and can carry bacteria.

Serves 6 to 8

8 ounces **Chinese pork sausage** *(or other sausage)*
1 pound **raw shrimp or prawns, peeled and deveined**
1 pound **sea scallops**
3 tablespoons **light soy sauce**
3 tablespoons **dry sherry**
1 whole **chicken breast, skinned, boned, and cut into bite-size pieces**
5 tablespoons **peanut oil**
1 **onion, finely diced**
2 cloves **garlic, very finely chopped**
2 teaspoons **grated fresh ginger**
2 pinches of **powdered saffron**
2 cups **basmati rice**
3 stalks **lemongrass, very finely chopped**
5 cups **Chicken Stock** *(see page 34)* or **seafood stock**
1/2 bunch **fresh Thai basil, finely chopped**
1 **red bell pepper, coarsely diced**
2 dozen **mussels, cleaned and beards removed**
1/2 cup **bean sprouts**

Cut the sausage into 1/4-inch slices. In a medium saucepan, sauté the sausage slices over medium-high heat until they are lightly seared and the fat has been rendered. Remove the sausage and place on paper towel to drain.

Toss the shrimp and scallops with 2 tablespoons of the soy sauce and 2 tablespoons of the sherry. In another small bowl, toss the chicken with the remaining 1 tablespoon each soy sauce and sherry.

In a large, deep frying pan, heat the oil over medium-high heat. Add the onion and sauté until just translucent. Add the garlic, ginger, and saffron, then add the rice and stir to coat well with the onion mixture, about 2 to 3 minutes. Add the lemongrass.

While stirring, gradually add the stock.. Turn the heat to high and allow the stock to come to a boil, then reduce to a medium simmer. Add the basil. Cook uncovered for 5 minutes. Add the chicken, sausage, and bell pepper. Cover and simmer for 15 minutes. Add the shrimp, scallops, and mussels, arranging them on top of the rice mixture. Sprinkle the bean sprouts on top of the seafood. Cover and cook for 5 to 8 minutes, until the shrimp and scallops are cooked and all mussels have opened.

Remove from the heat and allow to rest, still covered, for 5 more minutes. Gently toss the seafood and sprouts with the rice and serve.

BASIC GLUTEN DOUGH˅

Gluten is the part of wheat that contains protein; it is a significant source of protein in many Asian vegetarian diets. It's best to prepare gluten dough yourself, although it is available in a variety of ready-made forms, from large fresh slices in the refrigerated sections of Asian supermarkets to canned vegetarian stew preparations complete with other vegetables.

Makes 12 ounces

1 cup gluten flour
About ¹/₂ cup water

Place the gluten flour in a mixing bowl and add the water in small amounts until a dough is formed. The amount of water needed will vary, so judge by the dough itself. Keep your hands wet. Mix the dough well, then form into a ball, cover the bowl, and let rest for 30 minutes.

Bring a large pot of water to a boil. Shape the dough into any form you like. For this basic recipe, shape into a cylinder about 2 inches in diameter and then cut into "steaks" about ³/₄ inch thick. Drop the steaks into the boiling water, lower the heat to a simmer, cover, and cook for 30 minutes. The gluten steaks will swell to about three times their original size.

Drain in a colander and let cool. Squeeze gently to remove any excess water. Cover with plastic wrap and refrigerate. Use within 3 days.

SHREDDED GLUTEN WITH CASHEWS˅

Many temples, restaurants, and vegetarian homes utilize gluten as a meat substitute. There are even many clever ways of molding and flavoring it so that the dish actually looks and smells like a meat dish. Gluten dough can be used in any stir-fried dish: simply marinate and cook it as you would chicken or beef.

Here, the gluten replaces shredded chicken in a dish from Northern China.

Serves 4

8 ounces gluten dough (*see recipe at left*)
1 tablespoon canola oil
2 slices fresh ginger, slivered
2 cloves garlic, slivered
4 ounces red bell pepper, cut into julienne
4 ounces green beans, cut into julienne
1 tablespoon brown bean sauce
¹/₂ teaspoon chile oil
¹/₂ cup Vegetarian Stock (*see page 30*)
1 tablespoon light soy sauce
1 tablespoon cornstarch, mixed with a little water
4 ounces cashews, roasted or deep fried

Cut the gluten dough into strips to resemble shreds of meat.

Heat a nonstick pan and add the oil, ginger, and garlic. (Increase the amount of oil if using another type of pan.) Stir-fry for a few seconds, then add the red bell pepper and green beans. Cook until half-done: the beans should just turn to a darker green color, and the edges of the bell pepper should be slightly translucent. Remove from the pan.

Stir-fry the gluten strips over high heat, searing carefully. Then add the bean sauce, chile oil, stock, and soy sauce. Cover the pan. Lower the heat and simmer gently for 15 minutes.

Return the vegetables to the pan. Increase the heat and stir-fry until the color of the vegetables is bright and they are tender. If you want to thicken the sauce, push the vegetables to the sides of the pan when they are about 80 percent cooked, creating a "well" for the sauce in the center. Slowly add the cornstarch and water mixture, stirring constantly, until the sauce is as thick as you like. Turn the gluten strips and vegetables in the sauce a few times, and remove to plates. Sprinkle the cashews over the top.

Serve family style with rice, or make individual plates with beds of rice over which you spoon the gluten and vegetables.

STEAMED FISH

Steaming foods is one of the healthiest and most convenient ways to cook. No oil is needed, there is no chance of burning the foods, and all the nutrients are retained.

Many types of fish can be steamed. Try cod, catfish, tilapia, or even trout. A rounder, shorter fish like cod can be cooked whole, while a long fish, like a catfish or trout, should be cut into sections about 1 inch thick. If you can only get the steaks of a large fish, such as a salmon, you can still use this steaming method.

Serves 4

1 whole fish, about 2 pounds, cleaned
2 teaspoons soy sauce
2 tablespoons rice wine
3 slices fresh ginger, cut into slivers
2 green onions
Cilantro to garnish

Wash the fish thoroughly and remove any scales that may have been missed. Drain and pat dry. If cooking a whole fish, make three deep cuts on the body. Place the fish on a large, deep plate or shallow dish that is heatproof. If using sections or steaks of fish, place them cut side up. The plate must be big enough to accommodate the fish and deep enough to hold the liquid that will form around it. Sprinkle with the soy sauce, rice wine, and ginger. Marinate for at least 30 minutes.

Prepare a wok or large pot with a steaming rack that will hold the plate above 1 inch of water. Bring the water to a full boil, then place the plate holding the fish on top of the rack. Cover and steam for 20 minutes.

Cut the green onions into thin round slices. Remove the leaves from the cilantro stems.

Remove the plate from steamer. If serving family style, garnish with green onions and cilantro and bring directly to the table. If serving individually—best done when the fish is cut into small steaks—separate the individual pieces of fish, garnish, and spoon some of the juice from the plate onto each piece.

STEAMED CHICKEN

Steaming a chicken creates a quick and appealing main dish. It adds no extra fat, and allows the natural flavors to come through. This dish is frequently used for those who are recovering from illness because it is easy to digest and is full of flavor without being spicy.

Ham is optional, depending on your dietary preferences. The choice of ham has long been the object of passion and debate among Chinese cooks. Some have gone to great lengths to import ham from Virginia and prosciutto from Italy.

Serves 4

1 whole chicken, about 4 1/2 pounds
2 teaspoons soy sauce
2 tablespoons rice wine
5 slices fresh ginger
4 ounces cooked ham or prosciutto, cut into slivers *(optional)*
6 fresh shiitake mushrooms, sliced
2 green onions
Cilantro to garnish

Clean the chicken thoroughly, and cut it into legs and breasts. Using a large cleaver, chop it cleanly into smaller pieces, bones and all. Each piece should be the same size, about 1 1/4 inch thick. Small drumsticks and wings can be left whole. Arrange all the pieces cut side up in a deep plate or shallow dish that is heatproof. Sprinkle the soy sauce and rice wine over the chicken. Arrange the ginger slices over the chicken. If you want to have the flavor of the ham, arrange it over the chicken. Finally, add the mushrooms.

Prepare a wok or large pot with a steaming rack that will hold the plate above 1 inch of water. Bring the water to a full boil, then place the plate holding the chicken on top of the rack. Cover and steam for 20 minutes.

Remove the plate from the steamer. Discard the ginger slices. If serving family style, garnish with the green onions and cilantro and bring directly to the table. If serving individually, separate the pieces of chicken, garnish, and spoon some of the juice from the plate onto each piece.

PART 3

EAST-WEST FLAVORS

One of the great paradoxes of Zen has been the masters' rejection of scripture and yet their insistence on lifelong study. While this has led to a backward-looking attitude that has influenced the Zen approach to food, we can still be creative, even as we affirm our commitment to Zen cooking. We know what Zen cooking has been in the past. How will we develop it in the future?

The food in this section is the creation of Arnold Wong. His food is visually attractive and delicious. The dishes take inspiration from both Eastern and Western cooking, but emerge as well-balanced and thoughtful creations in their own right. They go beyond collage approach towards something whole and complete. Cooking that comes from a successful cross-fertilization of cultures can be a good metaphor. Just as East-West cooking must combine the elements of different cuisines without losing its integrity, Zen can exist in a multicultural world while maintaining its essential character.

Throughout the centuries, Zen masters have turned to secular experts. They have asked martial artists to improve the health of monks and teach them the means of self-defense. They have learned from potters about the lessons of craft. They have employed calligraphers, painters, poets, and musicians to enhance the creativity of temple residents. Another role of the Zen masters has been to preserve treasures and knowledge, and to serve as cultural arbiters. The Daitokuji temple, for example, has a priceless art collection, and Rikyu influenced generations of tea masters, garden designers, and collectors of folk art. In turn, creative people of all fields have engaged in an ongoing dialogue with their cultivated Zen friends.

In the same centuries-long tradition of exchange, we have turned to a master chef to suggest new directions Zen cooking might take. His food allows each ingredient to be discernible, blends them into a harmonious and fine-tasting whole, and presents them in colorful and thoughtful ways without contrivance. This should be the culinary goal of all Zen cooking.

PAN-ASIAN DASHI

This dashi includes Thai ginger as a contrast to the marine flavor of the seaweed. The konbu must be soaked overnight, so plan ahead when making this dish.

Makes about 3 quarts

1 pound konbu (*dried kelp*)
4 quarts cold water
¼ cup fresh galangal (*Thai ginger*), peeled and sliced into
⅛-inch pieces
8 ounces hana katsuo (*dried bonito flakes*)

Rinse the konbu, then soak it in the cold water overnight.
Place the konbu and water in a large pot and slowly bring to a simmer; do not allow it to boil. Add the galangal and simmer for 2 to 3 hours.
Add the bonito flakes and allow to simmer for a further 30 minutes.
Carefully strain through a fine conical sieve. Strain again through cheesecloth or muslin. Return to a clean pot and simmer to the desired consistency. Reducing the stock will concentrate its flavor.

MISO

There are many varieties of miso, ranging in color from white to a dark chocolate-brown and in taste from sweet to rich and salty. Miso is made by crushing boiled soybeans, mixing them with wheat, barley, or rice, and adding a yeastlike mold (koji) to induce fermentation. The resulting mixture is allowed to age from several weeks to as much as three years.

White miso (shiro or saikyo miso) is a specialty of Kyoto. It is made from soybeans and rice and not aged. It has a smooth consistency and a wonderful sweet, rich taste. White miso is the most commonly used miso in kaiseki cooking.

Beige miso (shinshu miso) is fairly salty with a delightfully tart taste. This is the miso that is most commonly available outside Japan.

Red miso (aka miso and hatcho miso) has a deep rich saltiness and robust flavor. In kaiseki, red miso is most often used during the summer months when salty flavors are most appreciated.

Miso is sold in small plastic tubs in the chilled section of Asian supermarkets. Price is often an indication of quality, especially for white and red miso. When buying white miso, always check the label and avoid any miso with additional ingredients such as barley or corn syrup (mizuame) and sake lees (sediment). Unfortunately, even in Japan, it is difficult to find good white miso outside of Kyoto. Try all the types of miso that are available to you and use your own good judgment.

TOMATO-MISO SOUP^v

Puréed soups are best when the ingredients are allowed to cook slowly, or sweat, to release all their flavors. When sweating vegetables, it is essential that the heat be kept low and that the vegetables are stirred regularly.

Use the best tomatoes you can find—late summer and autumn are the peak times. When good fresh tomatoes are unavailable, you can use canned ones.

Serves 8 to 10

¼ cup butter
1 tablespoon very finely chopped garlic
2 tablespoons very finely chopped fresh ginger
1 medium onion, chopped
1 bunch celery, white inner stalks only, chopped
1 carrot, chopped
½ cup mirin *(sweet rice wine)*
2½ pounds ripe tomatoes, seeded and chopped
½ cup red miso paste
3 cups Vegetarian Stock *(see page 30)*
¾ cup tomato paste *(optional)*
White pepper to taste

TO GARNISH
1 tomato, seeded and cut into julienne
1 bunch green onions, thinly sliced
½ cup crème fraîche, whipped to soft peaks
2 teaspoons very finely chopped fresh ginger

Melt the butter in a heavy-bottomed pot. Add the garlic, ginger, onion, celery, and carrot and sweat (cook over low heat) for 15 to 30 minutes, stirring constantly. Do not allow the vegetables to brown.

Deglaze with the mirin, stirring well. Add the tomatoes and sweat for a further 15 minutes.

Whisk in the miso paste. When all the ingredients are thoroughly mixed, slowly add the stock. Bring to a low simmer, then leave to cook for 45 minutes to 1 hour. If there isn't enough tomato flavor, add the tomato paste. Season with pepper to taste.

Remove from the heat and ladle into a blender or food processor. Be careful because the soup will be hot. Fill the blender no more than two-thirds at a time. Begin puréeing at low speed, increasing to a higher speed.

Pour the puréed soup into a conical sieve set over a clean pan to strain. Reheat if necessary. The soup may be simmered longer if a thicker consistency is desired. Adjust the seasoning. Garnish each serving with sliced green onions and tomato julienne. Combine the ginger and crème fraîche and add a dollop to each bowl of soup.

CREAM OF WATERCRESS AND ASIAN PEAR SOUP ᵛ

When you feel overheated or dehydrated, or if you have had too much fried food, this soup makes a delightful antidote. Watercress is thought to moisten and relieve the lungs, and Asian pear does the same. This soup is ideal in the time between summer and autumn, when the air begins to turn dry.

The Asian pear *(see opposite)* comes in several different varieties, and tastes like a cross between an apple and a pear. It can be eaten raw. The flesh should be crisp and full of juice. It is such a prized fruit that it is available dried as well as fresh, and is also used as a medicine in herbal formulas.

Other pears, such as Bartlett, William's, or French "butter" pears, can be substituted as long as they are very fragrant.

Serves 8

¼ **cup butter**
2 tablespoons canola oil
2 tablespoons very finely chopped garlic
1 medium yellow onion, chopped
3/4 cup celery, white inner stalks only, chopped
2 cups Asian pears, peeled and chopped
4 packed cups watercress, finely chopped
1 bunch fresh flat-leaf parsley, very finely chopped
1 1/2 packed cups spinach leaves
4 cups Vegetarian or light Chicken Stock (see pages 30 and 34)
1 cup heavy cream or milk
1/3 cup rice flour
Salt and white pepper, sugar or honey to taste

TO GARNISH
Crème fraîche, Sliced green onion

Melt the butter in a large pot, then add the oil. When the oil and butter are fully mixed, add the garlic, onion, and celery. Sweat for 15 to 20 minutes, stirring constantly to prevent the vegetables from coloring. Adjust the heat if necessary. Add the pears and cook for a further 10 minutes. Add the watercress, parsley, and spinach leaves. Cook until wilted. Add the stock. Bring quickly to a boil, then reduce to a simmer.

In a bowl, gradually whisk the rice flour into the cream until the mixture is smooth and of the desired consistency. Pour the cream mixture into the soup and bring back to a simmer, stirring.

Remove from the heat. Purée the soup, in small batches, in a blender or food processor. Pass the puréed soup through a conical sieve into a clean pan.

Reheat if necessary, then adjust the seasoning with salt, white pepper, and sugar to taste. Garnish each serving with a dollop of crème fraîche and sliced green onion.

LEEK AND SHIITAKE MUSHROOM SOUP^v

The addition of cream gives this soup a rich and velvety texture. Stir the soup just before serving, since the cream will rise to the top. A rich chicken stock, or a highly reduced vegetarian stock, is essential for this soup.

Serves 8 to 10

1 cup butter
2 tablespoons very finely chopped garlic
2 medium yellow onions, chopped
2 quarts leeks *(mostly white parts)*, chopped
6 to 8 fresh bay leaves
1/4 bunch fresh oregano leaves, very finely chopped
1 1/2 pounds fresh shiitake mushroom, stems removed and sliced
12 ounces cremini or chestnut mushrooms, sliced
4 cups Chicken Stock *(see page 34)*
2 cups heavy cream
2 teaspoons black pepper
Salt to taste

Melt the butter in a large heavy-bottomed pot. Add the garlic, onions, leeks, bay leaves, and oregano. Sweat, stirring constantly, on medium-high heat until the onions are translucent. If any of the vegetables start to color, reduce the heat. Add the mushrooms and cook until they begin to soften. Add the stock slowly, then bring to a boil and simmer for 15 to 20 minutes.

Add the cream and bring back to a simmer. Season with the pepper and salt to taste. Serve immediately with crusty bread.

ROASTED VEGETABLE-MISO SOUP^v

This soup is an Asian version of minestrone. Roasting the vegetables brings out the best of their flavor, while the addition of miso lends a hearty earthiness. There are several types of miso paste. Red miso has a pronounced bold flavor, while white miso is subtle and sweet.

Serves 6 to 8

A 4-ounce piece fresh ginger, cut into julienne
¼ cup garlic cloves, smashed
1 sweet yellow onion, diced
8 ounces fresh shiitake mushrooms, stems removed and sliced
½ small head green cabbage, napa cabbage, or bok choy, chopped into 1-inch squares
4 ounces carrots, cut into thick julienne
3 ounces turnips or daikon radish, diced
3 ounces rutabaga, diced
3 ounces potatoes, red and white, diced
2 tablespoons pure sesame oil
2 tablespoons canola oil
4 tablespoons soy sauce

1 teaspoon dried red chile flakes
1 teaspoon sesame seeds
½ cup dry sake
½ cup mirin *(sweet rice wine)*
6 cups Vegetarian or Chicken Stock *(see pages 30 and 34)*
5 fluid ounces miso paste, red or white
6 ounces zucchini, cut into ¼-inch dice
2 eggs
Salt and black pepper to taste

To garnish
2 sheets nori *(dried seaweed)*
Slivered green onions

Preheat oven to 400°F. Mix together the ginger, garlic, onion, shiitake mushrooms, cabbage, carrots, turnips, rutabaga, and potatoes in a large bowl. Toss with the oils, soy sauce, chile flakes, and sesame seeds. Place in a greased roasting pan and roast in the oven until lightly golden.

Remove the vegetables to a large pot. Deglaze the roasting pan with the sake and mirin, stirring well, then add the liquid to the pot. Add the stock and miso. Stir to dissolve the miso. The stock should just cover the vegetables. Quickly bring to a boil. Add the zucchini, then reduce to a simmer and simmer for 10 to 15 minutes.

Meanwhile, prepare the garnish. Toast the nori lightly by holding each sheet with tongs and passing it quickly over an open flame, about 5 to 10 seconds on each side. After toasting, cut the nori into fine strips. Set aside.

Lightly beat the eggs in a bowl with a fork.

Slowly drizzle the eggs into the simmering soup. When you move the spoon slowly through the soup, the eggs should set into ribbons. Season with salt and black pepper to taste. Garnish with the nori and green onions and serve immediately.

GINGER AND MANGO GAZPACHO^v

This is a light and refreshing soup that is perfect in warm weather. It should be made in late summer, when tomatoes are at their peak. Select tomatoes that are dark, firm, sweet, and vibrant in color.

Cans of chipotle peppers packed in a tomato-based sauce are available in Hispanic food markets. The sauce should be rinsed off before using the peppers.

Serves 10 to 12

3 pounds fresh, ripe tomatoes
4 to 12 tablespoons tomato paste *(optional)*
1/2 red onion, diced small
1 English cucumber, cut into short, thin julienne
3/4 cup celery, white inner stalks only, finely diced
8 ounces fresh shiitake mushrooms, stems removed and sliced
1 red bell pepper, diced small
1 green bell pepper or seeded pasilla chile, diced small
1 zucchini, diced small
1 bunch green onions, thinly sliced *(both white and green)*
1/2 bunch cilantro, very finely chopped
1 tablespoon rinsed and very finely chopped canned chipotles, or dried red chile flakes
1 large, firm mango, diced
4 cups light Vegetarian or Chicken Stock *(see pages 30 and 34)*
2 tablespoons lime juice
1 tablespoon lemon juice

2 tablespoons balsamic vinegar *(preferably at least 10 years old)*
1 tablespoon soy sauce

To SEASON
1 1/2 tablespoons cumin seeds, toasted and ground
2 tablespoons unsalted ancho chile powder or other mild chile powder
2 teaspoons black pepper
Salt to taste
Sugar or honey to taste
4 tablespoons light-tasting olive oil
2 tablespoons garlic, very thinly sliced on a mandoline
2 tablespoons very finely chopped fresh ginger

To GARNISH
Crème fraîche mixed with very finely chopped cilantro
Avocado slices

Core the tomatoes and score a cross on the bottom of each one. Bring a large pot of lightly salted water to a boil. Prepare an ice bath with half water and half ice. Quickly blanch the tomatoes in the boiling water, cooking only until the skins start to peel away from the scored crosses. The required time will be approximately 2 to 5 minutes. Immediately remove the tomatoes from the boiling water with a strainer and plunge into the ice bath. Peel the skins off the tomatoes. Cut them in half and squeeze out the seeds and excess pulpy liquid.

Purée one-sixth of the tomatoes in a blender. If the tomatoes you are using do not have a lot of flavor, add tomato paste to taste.

Chop the remaining tomatoes to a medium coarseness and put in a large bowl. Combine the purée with the chopped tomatoes.

Add all the remaining vegetables, then add the cilantro, chipotles, mango, stock, lime and lemon juices, vinegar, and soy sauce. Stir well. Season with the cumin, chile powder, pepper, salt, and sugar to taste.

Heat the oil in a pan until it begins to smoke. Lightly toast the garlic and ginger, then pour over the gazpacho. Chill the soup for at least 3 hours. (Chilling the soup overnight is the best method because it allows all the flavors to blend and become more subtle.) Add garnishes just before serving.

ROCK SHRIMP CAKES

Rock shrimp are usually bought already peeled and cleaned. You can also use other shrimp or prawns. Be sure to peel and devein them.

This recipe can be adapted for use with other types of shellfish, especially scallops, crab, and lobster.

Makes 10 cakes, 4 ounces each

1½ pounds peeled raw rock shrimp
1 medium red onion, very finely chopped
1 red bell pepper, very finely chopped
1 cup celery, white inner stalks only, very finely chopped
1 cup fresh water chestnuts, very finely chopped
½ bunch fresh flat-leaf parsley, very finely chopped
2 eggs
1 stalk lemongrass, very finely chopped, tough outer leaves removed
1 tablespoon very finely chopped fresh ginger
1 tablespoon very finely chopped garlic

At least 1 cup panko (*Japanese bread crumbs*)
1 tablespoon salt
1 teaspoon black pepper

FOR THE FLAVORED CREAM
1 cup heavy cream
2 stalks lemongrass, cut into 4-inch pieces and smashed
A 2-ounce piece fresh ginger, smashed
5 large cloves garlic, smashed

TO FINISH
About 4 cups panko, for breading
Oil for frying

Rinse the shrimp, discarding any remaining shells. Drain well and roughly chop. Combine with the onion, bell pepper, celery, water chestnuts, and parsley in a large bowl. Whisk the eggs and add to the mixture.

To make the flavored cream, heat the cream, lemongrass, ginger, and garlic in a heavy-bottomed saucepan. Simmer until the cream is reduced by half. Then remove from heat, strain, and cool.

Once the cream is cool, add it to the shrimp and mix well. Add the finely chopped lemongrass, ginger, and garlic and enough bread crumbs to bind the mixture. You will have to vary the amount according to the

moisture content of the shrimp; you should be able to pat the mixture into a firm ball. Season with salt and pepper.

Spread a thin layer of bread crumbs on a baking tray. Using a round biscuit cutter, about 2½ inches in diameter and ¾ inch high, as a mold, make individual cakes from the shrimp mixture. (Use an ice cream scoop to put the mixture into the mold.) Top with more crumbs and press firmly on each cake with a glass or can to flatten it. Chill the cakes for a minimum of 6 hours.

Shallow- or deep-fry the cakes until golden brown on both sides. Drain well and serve hot with Spicy Sriracha Aïoli.

SPICY SRIRACHA AÏOLI

Sriracha is a Vietnamese hot chile sauce found in most Asian markets. This delicious twist on basic aïoli can be used in many different ways, from an accompaniment for shrimp cakes to a spread for sandwiches.

Makes about 5 cups

2 eggs
1 egg yolk
2 tablespoons sugar
1 tablespoon Dijon mustard
1 tablespoon sriracha sauce
1½ tablespoons lemon juice
1 tablespoon distilled white vinegar
2 tablespoons grated fresh ginger, very finely chopped
2 teaspoons salt
1 teaspoon white pepper
About 6 cups canola or other light vegetable oil

Place the whole eggs, egg yolk, and sugar in a blender and blend on high until frothy.

Whisk the mustard, sriracha, lemon juice, vinegar, ginger, salt, and pepper together in a bowl. Add to the egg mixture in the blender. Blend on high to mix, then slowly drizzle in the oil in small portions until the aïoli begins to stiffen up in the blender.

RARE TUNA AND MANGO SPRING ROLLS

This delicious combination of Chinese and Japanese ingredients is a fresh version of a rather hackneyed restaurant dish.

It's worthwhile searching for tuna loin. Although tuna steaks may be used, the grain will not be parallel to the long sides of the sticks you will be cutting. As a result, the pieces will begin to fall apart and will lack the texture so integral to this dish.

The oil you use for deep-frying should be clean and fresh, and it must be at the correct temperature. Be sure to use a thermometer.

Makes 15 rolls

1 1/2 pounds #1 sushi-grade tuna loin
1/4 cup toragashi (Japanese chile powder) or cayenne pepper
1/3 cup black sesame seeds
2 tablespoons salt
2 large sheets nori (dried seaweed) for sushi, preferably toasted
1 very firm mango
1/2 bunch cilantro
1 egg
1 package Hong-Kong-style spring roll wrappers
Oil for deep-frying

Trim the tuna and portion into approximately 3-inch x 1/2-inch sticks weighing about 1 1/2 ounces each. Set aside.

Combine the chile powder, sesame seeds, and salt on a plate and spread out evenly. Cut the sheets of nori into quarters. Peel the mango and cut very thin slices from the widest part of the fruit, using a mandoline. Pull the cilantro sprigs off the stems. Beat the egg lightly in a small bowl.

Roll the tuna in the chile powder and sesame seed mixture until evenly coated. Place a single spring roll wrapper on a clean, dry surface. With one of the corners facing you, place a piece of nori horizontally on top of the wrapper, followed by two thin pieces of mango and a stick of tuna. Top with 2 to 3 sprigs of cilantro.

Using a pastry brush, moisten the edges of the wrapper with the beaten egg. (It is essential that you brush all edges if the roll is to be properly sealed.) Roll up the wrapper beginning with the point facing you. Bring both sides in as you pass the halfway point of rolling. You will finish with the point opposite you. Be sure the roll is well sealed so no oil will penetrate during frying. Make the remaining rolls in the same way.

Deep fry in oil heated to 350°F until the rolls are a light golden color all over. In order to prevent the oil temperature from dropping during frying, cook only two or three rolls at a time. Remove, drain, and cut immediately to prevent the tuna from overcooking.

Serve with a dipping sauce of your choice (see page 54).

SHIITAKE MUSHROOM RISOTTO^v

Since rice is such a central part of Asian meals, there are a huge variety of dishes where rice is the central ingredient. Some are as simple as mixing pieces of meat and sausage with rice as it is cooking. Other dishes begin with a sauté of mountain vegetables before cooking rice in the same pot. This recipe, and the Garlic Chive and Sweet Maui Onion Risotto that follows on page 92, marry Asian ingredients with Italian cooking methods. The risotto method incorporates all the nutrients from the other ingredients, making a dish that is easy to digest. Arborio rice has unique properties, and should be a staple in the cupboard of everyone who cooks with rice.

Serves 4 as a main dish

1 cup butter
1 clove garlic, very finely chopped
8 ounces shallots, chopped
1/2 bunch fresh oregano leaves, chopped
8 fresh bay leaves
1 pound fresh baby shiitake mushrooms
4 cups arborio rice
2 cups dry white wine
8 cups light Vegetarian or Chicken Stock
(see pages 30 and 34), heated to simmering
3/4 cup extra virgin olive oil
1/2 bunch fresh flat-leaf parsley
1 cup Parmesan cheese, freshly grated

Melt the butter in a heavy-bottomed pot, then add garlic, shallots, oregano, and bay leaves. Stirring with a wooden spoon, sauté until the shallots are translucent, about 5 to 7 minutes. Add the mushrooms and cook for 5 more minutes.

Add the rice and stir, making sure that all of the grains are well coated with butter. Pour in the wine and simmer until almost all of the wine has been absorbed, stirring constantly.

Add the hot stock slowly, a ladleful at a time, letting each be absorbed before adding the next. Simmer, stirring constantly, until the rice begins to get creamy and the grains are cooked to your desired tenderness. The amount of stock needed will vary with the quality of the rice. Add only as much stock as is needed.

Spoon the risotto onto serving plates. Drizzle with olive oil, and sprinkle with the parsley and Parmesan cheese. Serve immediately.

SPICY MANGO DIPPING SAUCE^v

This fruity, vibrantly colored dipping sauce is very versatile. It goes well with the Rare Tuna and Mango Spring Rolls *(see page 88)*, and is also a fine accompaniment to all sorts of grilled fish dishes.

Makes about 2 cups

2 large mangoes, flesh puréed
3 fluid ounces rice vinegar
Juice of 2 lemons
4 tablespoons canola oil
4 tablespoons very finely chopped cilantro
4 tablespoons very finely chopped fresh Thai basil leaves
2 tablespoons very finely chopped fresh mint leaves
1 tablespoon very finely chopped fresh ginger
2 teaspoons very finely chopped garlic
1/4 cup honey
2 tablespoons palm sugar or soft brown sugar
1 teaspoon toragashi *(Japanese chile powder)* or cayenne pepper

Combine all the ingredients in a food processor or blender and blend well.

GARLIC CHIVE AND SWEET MAUI ONION RISOTTO

Garlic chives *(see opposite)*, long used in Asia, have only recently begun to appear in Western markets. They have a subtle flavor and firm texture, and are an important element in northern Chinese dishes. Sweet onions make an excellent companion to the chives.

Larger quantities of the risotto can be cooked ahead of time if necessary. When reheating, add a little more chicken stock and season as needed.

Serves 4 as a main dish

1 cup butter
4 cups Maui or other sweet white onions, diced
1/4 cup garlic cloves, crushed
1 bunch fresh thyme leaves, very finely chopped
8 fresh bay leaves

4 cups arborio rice
2 cups white wine
8 cups Chicken Stock *(see page 34)*, heated to simmering
Salt and black pepper to taste
2 cups garlic chives, chopped

Melt the butter in a heavy-bottomed pot and sauté the onions, garlic, thyme, and bay leaves until the onions are translucent. Add the rice and stir well.

Pour in the wine and simmer until it is almost all absorbed, stirring constantly. Add the hot stock a little at a time, letting each addition be absorbed before adding the next. Keep stirring. The rice must retain a slightly firm bite, so do not overcook.

Season the risotto with salt and pepper. Add the chives just before serving.

SPICY PONZU SAUCE^v

Traditionally, this sauce consists of soy sauce and lemon juice. This version adds spicier ingredients. It goes well with foods ranging from raw oysters to deep-fried vegetable spring rolls. In addition to being simple to make, it adds an intriguing flavor.

Makes 1 cup

4 tablespoons soy sauce
4 tablespoons Japanese plum wine
4 tablespoons mirin *(sweet rice wine)*
4 tablespoons fresh lemon juice

1 teaspoon very finely chopped garlic
1 teaspoon very finely chopped fresh ginger
1/2 teaspoon toragashi *(Japanese chile powder)* or cayenne pepper

Whisk all the ingredients together, blending well.

LEMONGRASS RISOTTO^v

All of Zen cooking relies upon on the quality of the ingredients. In this recipe, it is important that the arborio rice and the fish sauce be the best you can obtain. All risottos require another Zen quality: constant attention. If you lapse, the rice will stick. If you are constant, you will be rewarded with a wonderfully fragrant risotto. This goes well with the Blackened Asian Catfish on page 102.

Fish sauce is a gift from Vietnamese and Thai cooking that has quickly been adopted by other cuisines. It is made from anchovies that are fermented in brine, and is used much like soy sauce. It is pungent and salty. Use it sparingly at first and never straight from the bottle by itself—it is almost always used as part of a dip or sauce, or as a seasoning. It is essential to buy the premium grade. (In Vietnamese markets, look for the phrase nuoc nhi, which means premium grade.) The flavor must be clean, with no unpleasant aftertaste.

Fish sauce can add variety to your repertoire of flavors, but using it can take some practice. You might first try using it in the same way you'd use soy sauce. You can also experiment by creating new dipping sauces, using fish sauce as one of the main ingredients.

Lime leaves are also known as makrut or kaffir lime leaves. They have delicious floral and citrus aromas.

Serves 4 as a side dish

¹/₂ cup butter
2 medium yellow onions, chopped medium fine
6 garlic cloves, crushed
1 thumb-size piece fresh ginger, sliced
2 thumb-size pieces galangal (Thai ginger, see opposite), sliced
3 to 4 stalks lemongrass, outer leaves trimmed and cut into 3-inch pieces
2 sprigs fresh lime leaves
4 fresh bay leaves
2 cups arborio rice

1 cup white wine
Grated zest and juice of 2 limes
Grated zest and juice of 1 lemon
4 tablespoons fish sauce (omit for vegetarian version)
1 cup clam juice (if cooking vegetarian, use additional stock instead)
3 cups Vegetarian Stock (see page 30) or fish stock, heated to simmering
2 teaspoons black pepper
Salt to taste
Freshly grated Parmesan cheese

Melt the butter in a large heavy-bottomed pot and add the onions, garlic, ginger, galangal, lemongrass, and lime and bay leaves. Sweat over low heat, stirring constantly, until the onions are translucent. Do not let them brown.

Add the rice and stir to coat all the grains with butter. Pour in the wine and simmer until it is almost all absorbed, stirring constantly. Add the citrus zest and juices and the fish sauce. Then add the clam juice and bring to a boil, stirring constantly. The rice will become creamy. Add the hot stock a little at a time, letting each addition be absorbed before adding the next. (The actual amount of stock required will vary with the quality of the rice.) Continue to stir while cooking, until the rice is tender but retains an inner crunch.

Season to taste and remove from the heat. Garnish with Parmesan cheese and serve immediately.

RED RICE STIR-FRY^v

Red rice was such a rarity in imperial China that most of it was sent to the emperor. Aside from its flavor, its color was undoubtedly part of its appeal—red is a symbol of good luck and is also associated with cinnabar, one of the legendary ingredients in the elixir of immortality. This dish is made even more unusual by the use of Camargue red rice. Camargue red rice is a medium-grain rice, organically grown in the south of France. If you cannot find this rice, you can substitute brown rice or wild rice. For the stir-fried vegetables, try fresh shiitake mushrooms, peppers, and peas. Experiment with your favorite combinations for wonderful new flavors.

You could also make this recipe richer with the addition of scallops, shrimp, or prawns.

Serves 4

2 cups Camargue red rice
4 tablespoons canola oil
3 cups stir-fried vegetables *(see above)*, **cut into bite-size pieces**
1 cup Vegetarian or Chicken Stock *(see pages 30 and 34)*

FOR THE SAUCE
1 cup dry sherry
4 tablespoons arrowroot
1 cup sweet sherry or light-tasting port
1/2 cup oyster sauce
4 tablespoons soy sauce
3 tablespoons lemon juice
3 tablespoons red wine vinegar
2 tablespoons Sambal Chile Sauce *(see page 99)*
2 tablespoons fish sauce
1 tablespoon very finely chopped fresh ginger
10 large garlic cloves, thinly sliced *(a mandoline is very good for this)*
1/4 bunch cilantro, very finely chopped

Cook the rice. Cool and set aside in a bowl.

Combine all the ingredients for the sauce in another bowl, whisking to mix in the arrowroot. Set aside.

Heat the oil in a well-seasoned or nonstick pan over high heat. Just before the oil begins to smoke, rapidly stir-fry the vegetables. If you are preparing this with the addition of seafood, stir-fry the seafood first, then stir-fry the vegetables before returning the seafood to the pan.

Add the rice and continue to stir-fry briefly. Add the stock, cover, and allow the rice to steam.

When most of the liquid has evaporated, stir the sauce well and add to the pan. Toss all the ingredients quickly as the sauce thickens. Serve immediately.

CHINESE STICKY RICE

This recipe is quite easy to prepare, but the rice does require soaking overnight. Traditionally, the rice is wrapped up in a lotus leaf and steamed; the lotus leaves infuse the rice with a tealike quality.

The usual steaming apparatus for the rice is a covered Chinese bamboo steamer set on top of a wok. However, contemporary steamers in a double-boiler arrangement work equally well.

Makes enough stuffing for 2 average-size chickens

4 cups sweet glutinous rice
3 fluid ounces light soy sauce
4 tablespoons dark soy sauce
4 tablespoons oyster sauce
2 tablespoons pure sesame oil
8 ounces Chinese sausage, sliced
5½ ounces small fresh shiitake mushrooms, stems removed and sliced
4 ounces fresh water chestnuts, peeled and sliced
1 bunch green onions, thinly sliced
¼ bunch cilantro, very finely chopped
1 tablespoon black sesame seeds

Rinse the rice and soak in cold water overnight.

Line a steamer with cheesecloth or muslin and steam the rice until it just turns translucent—approximately 20 to 25 minutes. Turn twice with a spoon during the steaming process for even cooking. Remove the rice to a baking sheet or plate to cool.

In a large bowl, combine the soy sauces, oyster sauce, and sesame oil. Add the sausage, mushrooms, water chestnuts, green onions, and cilantro and toss together until well mixed. Add the rice and combine well with your hands. Finally, add the sesame seeds.

Stuff into the cavity of a quail or chicken that has been tunnel boned (the ribcage and backbone removed, but leg and wing bones left in). Season and roast accordingly.

Serve the remaining stuffing on the side or portion into leaves of your choice and steam. Garnish with extra green onions.

GRILLED QUAIL STUFFED WITH CHINESE STICKY RICE

In the traditional version of this dish, the quail are deep-fried. This contemporary version has much more flavor and looks beautiful on the plate.

Tunnel-boning quail—removing the ribcage and backbone but not the leg and wing bones—is a job best left to the expert. Happily, quails boned this way can be bought from good butchers and many supermarkets.

Serves 4 to 6

12 quail, tunnel boned
Chinese Sticky Rice *(see opposite)*

Preheat the oven to 350°F. Stuff the quail with the Chinese Sticky Rice (see recipe at left).

Mark and sear the quail over a charcoal fire or on a preheated ridged cast-iron grill pan. Finish cooking in the oven for 15 to 20 minutes.

Serve with rice and stir-fried vegetables.

SPICY PAN-FRIED CHINESE LONG BEANS^v

This recipe also works well for vegetables like okra, sugarsnap peas, or snow peas. There will be some sauce left over, which should be saved and used as a sauce for stir-frying with other ingredients. Using a nonstick pan will mean that you use less oil.

Serves 6

**3/4 cup canola oil
3 pounds Chinese long beans, cut into
4-inch pieces**

**For the sauce
3/4 cup soy sauce
1/2 cup oyster sauce
2 tablespoons high-quality fish sauce
4 tablespoons white vinegar
4 tablespoons dry sherry
1/4 cup soft brown sugar
4 tablespoons honey
1/2 bunch fresh basil leaves, very
finely chopped
1/4 bunch fresh mint leaves, very
finely chopped
1/3 bunch cilantro, very finely chopped
2 to 3 fresh hot chiles, very finely chopped
1 tablespoon garlic, very finely chopped or
very thinly sliced
1 tablespoon fresh ginger, very
finely chopped
2 tablespoons Sambal Chile Sauce
(see right)
Grated zest of 1 lime
Juice of 3 limes
2 teaspoons black pepper
2 teaspoons dried red chile flakes**

**To garnish
Tomato slices
Green onions**

Whisk the sauce ingredients together and set aside.

In a large, preferably nonstick frying pan, heat half of the oil until it just begins to smoke. Add the long beans and stir-fry for 5 to 7 minutes. The beans will turn a bright green color. Add more oil if necessary.

Drain off excess oil and return the beans to the hot pan. Pour in the sauce and toss until the long beans are well coated. The sauce should begin to thicken and caramelize lightly after about 5 minutes.

Garnish with tomato slices and green onions. Serve immediately.

HOMEMADE SAMBAL CHILE SAUCE^v

If you like to use chile sauce in your everyday cooking, either as an ingredient or condiment, then this is an essential sauce to make and keep in your refrigerator. The flavors will change and develop even further during storage. Unlike store-bought sambal oelek, the Indonesian chile sauce, your homemade sauce won't contain any preservatives. For prolonged storage, keep your sambal in the freezer.

If jalapeños are unavailable, other red chiles can be substituted. It's best to use red chiles that are medium-hot.

Makes approximately 2 cups

**1 pound fresh red jalapeños
3/4 cup garlic cloves, peeled
1/2 cup white distilled vinegar
Sugar to taste
Salt to taste**

Remove the stems from the peppers and split them lengthwise. Remove half of the seeds. Place the peppers in a food processor fitted with a sharp blade and process until ground fairly fine.

Transfer to a blender. Add the garlic and blend until fairly smooth. Add vinegar to desired taste and consistency. (Depending on the type of chile you are using, the amount of liquid released will vary. The consistency of the sauce will thus vary as well, and the amount of vinegar added should be adjusted according to both taste and desired consistency.) Season with salt and sugar to taste.

GRILLED MISO-MARINATED SALMON

Both salmon and soy have considerable health benefits—salmon is rich in omega fatty acids, and there is evidence that soy helps prevent cancer. This recipe specifically uses white miso paste because it has the most subtle flavor of all the different types of miso.

Serves 6

**6 pieces of salmon fillet, 8 ounces each, sliced vertically *(salmon steaks may be substituted)*
2 to 3 Roma or large plum tomatoes, seeded and cut into julienne
1/4 bunch cilantro leaves
1 bunch green onions, thinly sliced**

For the marinade
**1 cup white miso paste
1 cup mirin *(sweet rice wine)*
1/2 cup canola oil
2 tablespoons garlic, very finely chopped
2 tablespoons fresh ginger, very finely chopped
2 teaspoons black pepper**

Whisk together the miso paste, mirin, oil, garlic, ginger, and pepper in a shallow dish. Add the salmon and turn to coat. Marinate in the refrigerator for a minimum of 4 hours.

If grilling over charcoal, clean the grill well, and oil it thoroughly to prevent sticking. The fire must be very hot. Grill for 5 to 7 minutes on each side, depending on the thickness of the fillets. Do not overcook. The fish can also be cooked indoors under the broiler.

Garnish with the tomatoes, cilantro leaves, and sliced green onions and serve.

OIL-CURED OLIVE AND MANGO PASTA ˅

This dish is made by tossing the sauce, which is rather like a tapenade, with cooked and cooled pasta. The sauce is quite versatile, and can also be used as a simple dip.

This pasta can also be served hot—prepare the sauce first and toss it with the hot pasta immediately after draining.

Serves 4

**1 pound short fresh pasta shapes, such as fusilli
2 tablespoons canola oil
1 large, firm mango, diced small
Parmesan cheese shavings**

For the sauce
**1 cup pitted Moroccan oil-cured olives, very finely chopped
1 medium red bell pepper, diced small
1 red onion, very finely chopped
3 to 4 green onions, thinly sliced
1/4 bunch cilantro, very finely chopped
Grated zest and juice of 1 lemon
2 tablespoons garlic, very finely chopped
1 tablespoon fresh ginger, very finely chopped
2 tablespoons dry sherry
4 tablespoons olive oil
2 teaspoons black pepper
Salt to taste
4 ounces tomato, diced**

Cook the pasta until al dente. Drain and allow to cool. Toss lightly with the canola oil.

Combine all the sauce ingredients and toss gently, then fold in the diced mango. Toss the mango and sauce together with the pasta. Serve with freshly shaved Parmesan cheese and tomatoes.

SAKE AND LEMONGRASS-STEAMED CHERRYSTONE CLAMS

The ancients believed that wine had a spirit (besides the obvious pun in English). Indeed, the word for qi, meaning both breath and the force of life, is a picture of fumes rising from fermenting rice. Here we have a dish that has the spirit of sake, the scent of lemongrass, and the aroma of the sea. The addition of coconut milk makes the broth lusciously rich.

The lemongrass-infused sake is made by steeping 4 to 5 stalks of lemongrass in a 720ml bottle for at least a week.

When selecting your clams, be sure they are fresh: check that they have a sweet seasalt smell, and that they close when poked.

Serves 2

3 pounds cherrystone or Manila clams, or other medium hard-shell clams
1 cup lemongrass-infused sake (see above)
2 stalks lemongrass, cut into 3-inch pieces
8 to 12 cloves garlic, crushed
1 tablespoon fresh black peppercorns, cracked

8 fresh bay leaves
1½ cups Chicken Stock (see page 34) or clam juice
8 to 12 fresh basil leaves, cut into thin shreds
Salt to taste
2 tablespoons butter or 2 tablespoons extra virgin olive oil
1 cup coconut milk (optional)

Wash the clams under cold running water. Discard any which do not close when tapped, as they will be dead, and may carry bacteria. Place them in a clay pot or frying pan along with the sake, lemongrass, garlic, bay leaves, and pepper. Bring to a boil, then reduce the liquid by half over high heat. Be careful that the alcohol does not flame.

Add the stock and basil. Salt to taste. Toss the clams once or twice. The clams must be rotated from top to bottom to cook evenly. If the clams are still closed, cover tightly and steam until they open. After steaming, discard any that have not opened, as closed cooked clams will not be fit for consumption.

Finish with the butter or oil and optional coconut milk. Pour the clams into a deep serving bowl or serve from the clay pot. Serve with crusty bread.

BLACKENED ASIAN CATFISH

There is a famous Zen painting showing a man with a gourd standing on the shore, gazing at a catfish in the water. From this odd juxtaposition, we are supposed to learn an important spiritual lesson.

With farm-raised fish becoming a larger part of the food supply, catfish makes a firm and tasty meal. If catfish is unavailable, snapper, grouper, or other firm-fleshed white fish can be substituted.

Serves 6

6 catfish fillets, 10 ounces each
½ cup soy sauce
3 fluid ounces dry sherry
2 tablespoons Sambal Chile Sauce (see page 99)
4 tablespoons pure sesame oil
4 tablespoons canola oil
4 tablespoons fresh ginger, very finely chopped
6 tablespoons garlic, very finely chopped
1 tablespoon fresh jalapeños, very finely chopped

Grated zest of 2 lemons
2/3 cup fermented black beans
½ bunch cilantro, including stems, very finely chopped
1 tablespoon dried red chile flakes
1 tablespoon five-spice powder
2 teaspoons black pepper
Salt to taste
1 cup peanut or canola oil for frying

Wash the fish fillets and pat dry. Combine all the remaining ingredients except for the peanut oil and add the fish fillets. Marinate in the refrigerator for a minimum of 3 hours. When you're ready to cook the fish, drain and discard the marinade. Preheat oven to 400°F.

Heat the peanut oil in a flameproof baking pan until it begins to smoke. Carefully place the fillets in the hot oil, skin side up. On a medium-high flame, cook for approximately 3 to 5 minutes or until the fish turns golden brown. Turn the fillets over. Cover, reduce the heat to medium, and cook for a further 5 to 7 minutes.

Finish cooking the fish in the oven for 10 to 15 minutes. Catfish should be fully cooked to avoid a rubbery texture. You can test this by pushing down on the middle of the fillets; they should be firm.

Remove from the pan. Pat dry on paper towels to remove excess oil. Serve immediately.

SAKE-STEAMED NEW ZEALAND GREEN-LIPPED MUSSELS

Meyer lemons have a fuller, sweeter, and more delicate flavor than regular lemons. However, they are available only at limited times commercially, so if they are not available, ordinary lemons can be used instead—just use less juice or add more honey, to taste.

If New Zealand green-lipped mussels are not available, black mussels can be substituted. Remember to buy fresh mussels and test by checking that they retract when poked, and have a sweet seasalt smell. Dead shellfish deteriorate quickly and can carry bacteria.

Serves 4

4 ounces fresh ginger, cut into 1/8-inch slices
5 1/2 ounces galangal *(Thai ginger),* cut into 1/8-inch slices
12 to 14 garlic cloves, crushed
6 fresh bay leaves
1 tablespoon fresh black peppercorns, cracked
2 teaspoons salt
1 1/2 cups sake
3 pounds New Zealand green-lipped mussels, scrubbed and beards removed
About 3 pounds ice, in small cubes or crushed
1 pound mixed baby lettuces

FOR THE MEYER LEMON VINAIGRETTE
1 cup Meyer lemon juice
3 tablespoons honey
5 1/2 tablespoons extra virgin olive oil

TO GARNISH
Sprigs of cilantro
Tomatoes

Place the ginger, galangal, garlic, bay leaves, peppercorns, and salt in a large pot and add the sake. Slowly bring to a boil. Add the cleaned mussels (which you should have checked for freshness), cover, and steam. Periodically stir the mussels, bringing the ones at the bottom to the top so that all will cook evenly. Check to see when the mussels open. Once they have all opened, drain in a colander. After steaming, discard any that have not opened.

Pour ice over the mussels to chill. Use just enough ice to cover all the mussels. Avoid excess water, which will dilute the steamed-in flavors. Remove from the ice as soon as the mussels are cool.

Serve the mussels on a bed of mixed baby lettuces dressed with the Meyer lemon vinaigrette, made by whisking the ingredients together. Garnish with cilantro sprigs and tomatoes.

SWEET SAKE-BRAISED CHICKEN LEGS

Many Asians believe that eating a certain part of an animal fortifies that part of the person who consumes it. Whether this is merely psychological or whether there is actual physical evidence, eating chicken legs is believed to be helpful to anyone dependent upon healthy legs—farmers, athletes, and even meditators. In fact, with the amount of meditation required by Zen, the health and circulation of blood through the legs is an ongoing concern.

Chicken legs are juicier than the breast meat, and have a fuller flavor. They are also quite economical, and are a good alternative to cooking a whole chicken.

This dish goes well with the Garlic Chive and Sweet Maui Onion Risotto on page 92.

Serves 6

**6 jumbo chicken legs, about 12 to 14 ounces each, thigh
bone removed
4 ounces galangal *(Thai ginger)*, sliced
4 ounces fresh ginger, sliced
6 garlic cloves, crushed
5 fresh bay leaves
1 tablespoon fresh black peppercorns, cracked
Salt to taste
2 cups sake
1 1/2 cups mirin *(sweet rice wine)*
2 cups Chicken Stock *(see page 34)*
1/2 cup soy sauce**

Preheat the oven to 275°F. Place the chicken legs skin side up in a large, lightly oiled roasting pan. Put the pan over a burner. Add the galangal, ginger, garlic, bay leaves, peppercorns, and salt. Add the sake to the pan. Bring to a boil and reduce by half. Add the mirin. Bring back to a boil and reduce by half. Add the stock and bring to a boil but do not reduce. Season with the soy sauce.

Cover the pan and place in the oven. The time needed to cook the chicken will vary considerably, depending on the size of the legs and the type of oven—it should take anywhere from 3 to 4 hours. The best way to judge if the chicken is done is if the fat has been rendered and the meat is just pulling away from the bone.

Remove from the oven and cool to room temperature. Remove the chicken legs from the pan and set aside. Skim the fat from the pan juices and strain. Serve the braising liquid with the chicken.

ASIAN-SPICED DUCK LEG CONFIT

Duck is one of the greatest and most popular delicacies of China, and is cooked in many ways, ranging from the famous Peking duck to a stewed version with herbs. The duck is a symbol in Buddhist ritual because it is a homonym for another word meaning the suppression of evil. It is also part of many Chinese embroideries and folk art—a duck in the reeds is a symbol of success in examinations, and the mandarin duck signifies a happy marriage, because mandarin ducks mate for life. Medicinally, duck is used to build vitality and is also used to treat edema. However, it should be used sparingly as too much of it is said to lead to an imbalance of dampness in the body.

This duck confit uses Asian spices. The duck legs should smell fresh, the flesh should be bright in color, and the skin must be moist and white. You can get extra duck fat from your butcher, or you can save the fat from whole ducks or chickens you may be using in other recipes.

This dish is prepared in advance and then stored, which makes it quite convenient. The reheated duck is delicious.

Serves 6 to 12

4 tablespoons salt
4 tablespoons five-spice powder
12 large duck legs, about 12 to 14 ounces each, thigh bone removed
12 to 16 garlic bulbs, halved horizontally
4 to 5 thumb-size pieces fresh ginger, cut into 1/4-inch slices
Peel from 2 oranges, sliced into strips
2 tablespoons black peppercorns
2 tablespoons white peppercorns
2 tablespoons Sichuan peppercorns
9 to 12 pieces star anise
12 to 16 dried hot red chiles
4 pounds duck or chicken fat (or just enough to cover)

Preheat the oven to 275°F. Sift the salt and five-spice powder together.

Trim the duck legs of excess fat, then season with the five-spice and salt mixture. Toss with the garlic, ginger, orange peel, peppercorns, star anise, and whole chiles.

Place in a deep roasting pan, skin side up, and cover with the duck fat. Cover the pan with aluminum foil. Cook in the oven for 2 1/2 to 3 hours. As the fat melts, be sure there is enough to cover the top of the legs. If not, add more fat.

Remove from the oven. There will be a large volume of hot fat, so be careful. Allow to cool, then refrigerate. The confit can be stored for several months as long as the fat covers the meat completely.

Remove from the fat when ready to use, and scrape off the spices and any remaining fat. Grill over charcoal, cook under the broiler, or place in a roasting pan, cover with aluminum foil, and heat in a preheated 300°F oven for 3 to 3 1/2 hours.

Serve with a vegetable purée or stir-fried greens.

BELGIAN ALE-MARINATED SKIRT STEAK

For those followers of Zen who are not vegetarian, red meat builds blood, muscle, and vitality. During the harsh winter months, a little red meat in one's diet can aid in resistance to the cold.

This marinade can be used on other cuts of meat, such as flank or rib-eye steak. Quick cooking on a hot grill creates a great flavor without overcooking the meat.

This may seem like a large amount of marinade, but it is difficult to achieve the proper proportions in a smaller batch. You can mix up a batch and use part of it for the marinade, then save the rest for another time, or use it for a sauce. However, you should not try to save the liquid after you've marinated the beef in it since it would have become mixed with the raw meat juices.

Serves 6

3 pounds skirt steak

FOR THE MARINADE
1 cup dark, full-bodied Belgian ale, such as Duval or Chimay
1½ cups Dijon mustard
1 cup olive oil
1 cup soy sauce
1 cup honey
4 tablespoons Worcestershire sauce
6 to 8 large fresh tomatoes, seeded and finely chopped
4 tablespoons lime juice

½ bunch fresh thyme leaves, very finely chopped
Grated zest of 2 limes
½ bunch fresh oregano leaves, very finely chopped
1 bunch cilantro, including stems, very finely chopped
1 bunch green onions, thinly sliced
¾ cup garlic cloves, very finely chopped
10 to 12 fresh bay leaves
1 tablespoon dried red chile flakes
4 tablespoons unsalted, dark, mild chile powder
2 teaspoons cayenne pepper
1 tablespoon black peppercorns, cracked

Mix together the marinade ingredients in a large bowl.

The thick, fatty membrane and most of the fat should have been trimmed from the steak by the butcher. If not, hold down the steak on a cutting board and pull the membrane away. It should peel away easily. Trim off the larger pieces of fat. The marbled fat will lend flavor to the beef and melt off during grilling.

Divide the steak into serving portions and arrange in a shallow dish. Whisk the marinade and pour over the steaks. Make sure that the steaks are well coated. Allow to marinate in the refrigerator for 4 to 6 hours. If you want to marinate for more than 6 hours, omit the lime juice from the marinade—the acids in the lime juice will begin to denature the protein in the steaks after 6 hours, and their texture will suffer.

Grill over a very hot charcoal fire, or on a preheated ridged cast-iron grill pan, for about 4 to 6 minutes per side, depending on the thickness of each strip of skirt steak.

ZEN

PART 4

TEA FLAVORS

After water drawn from a living spring, no drink complements the Zen meal better than tea. It is a natural, healthy drink that aids in digestion and enhances alertness. The enjoyment of tea has engendered many rituals, from a cup of tea drunk by a bright window to the contemplative gathering of the Zen-inspired tea ceremony. Tea is health, it is pleasure, it is friendship, and it is meditation.

TEA

The earliest use of tea is shrouded in myth. Like many ancient legends, however, these myths can provide important metaphors for understanding the significance of tea.

One Chinese legend asserts that tea was discovered by the emperor Shen Nong in 3000 b.c.e. It is said that he was boiling water when some leaves fell into the pot. He liked the drink and discerned that it had medicinal value. Indeed, Shen Nong is credited with the discovery of so many different herbal remedies and agricultural methods that he is also known as the Divine Cultivator.

Another legend concerns the twenty-eighth Zen patriarch and the person who brought Zen to China, Bodhidharma. After his arrival in China, he spent nine years facing a wall in constant meditation. When he fell asleep one day, he cut off his eyelids and cast them to the ground, and two tea plants instantly sprang up.

These two legends indicate two of the most important properties of tea. First, tea is a healthy drink. Its moderate amount of caffeine (depending on the type of tea and length of time brewed, tea contains about 20 to 50 percent of the caffeine content of coffee) stimulates the nervous system and promotes blood circulation. It enhances elimination and its diuretic qualities aid the kidneys. The essential oils in tea augment digestion and emulsify fat, one reason why so much tea is consumed during oily meals. It is an excellent source of nutrients, including vitamins C and E. Green tea has been shown to promote overall good health by lowering cholesterol, reducing blood pressure, and supporting the immune system.

Secondly, tea enhances alertness, and that is beneficial to a follower of Zen. Certainly, the health benefits and caffeine content are important factors. As Shen Nong is said to have written: "Tea induces a lightness of spirit, clarity of mind, and freedom from any sense of constriction." Many Buddhist and Taoist meditators throughout history have used tea to keep their minds clear. One story about the tea known as Tieguanyin, or the Iron Goddess of Mercy tea, tells of monks drinking it to keep them awake during long hours of meditation.

The many Japanese Zen masters who traveled to China to learn Buddhism also brought back Chinese poetry, calligraphy, music, and the Song dynasty style of tea. This style of tea became the basis for chanoyu— the tea ceremony—where powdered green tea is whisked to a froth in handmade tea bowls.

Eventually, the Chinese practice of tea evolved in different directions. The powdered and whisking methods died out, and were replaced by the steeping of whole leaves. Tea connoisseurs in China have come to prize varietal tea leaves. By contrast, Japan has both the steeping method and the powdered tea method. Powdered teas are usually blended from several varieties to achieve bright colors and subtle flavors.

Today, as we consider tea in the context of Zen cooking, we have the good fortune of having several methods of brewing tea available to us.

THE COVERED BOWLⱽ

One of the simplest and most casual ways to brew tea also happens to be the method favored by tea connoisseurs. They use a special bowl with a lid and saucer, but you can do the same thing with a rice bowl and put a saucer on top. Using a covered bowl allows you to brew just enough tea for one person, and it retains the flavor and bouquet very nicely. If you use a white porcelain tea bowl, you can judge the color and clarity of the tea before drinking, and you can also judge the quality of the leaves afterwards as well.

Chinese tea is roughly divided into four categories: green, black, white, and flowered teas. The pursuit of fine tea can become as obsessive as the pursuit of fine wine, but a beginner can find great pleasure in starting with these few teas:

LONGJING (Dragon Well): to many, the premier green tea, with a fresh grassy flavor.
OOLONG (Black Dragon): a semi-fermented tea with a toasted flavor.
PU-ER (name of a region in China): a fermented tea that brews very dark and has an earthy flavor.
XIANGPIAN (Jasmine): a green tea scented with jasmine flowers.

A tea connoisseur always examines the quality of the tea before brewing and often does a quick evaluation of the leaves after drinking the tea as well: are the leaves whole and undamaged by insects or poor handling? Are they the proper size for that type of tea? What position on the branch were they? (A high grade of Tieguanyin tea, for example, consists only of the third leaves from the tips; the highest grade of Longjing consists only of the bud and one leaf.) Are there many pieces of stem and other debris? (In the highest grades, there will only be the pure whole leaf, while in the cheapest grades, there will be broken leaves and stems, as well as pieces of grass and leaves of other plants.)

Some tea enthusiasts prefer to steep their green tea at lower temperatures—they are afraid of "cooking" their tea (green tea that has been heated for too long will look yellow instead of a clear green), so they leave the cover off. Others eschew this, saying that leaving the cover off allows the qi to escape. You are encouraged to try for yourself and decide.

The covered bowl method appears to be very casual. Some tea and hot water and proper steeping seem to be all that is needed. In a sense, this is tea brewing at its most basic. Yet it is also a favored way for those who will subject the tea to far more scrutiny than the average person. It is, in a sense, a summation of the whole love of tea: what can begin with immediate enjoyment can become a lifetime of exploration and appreciation.

1 teaspoon tea leaves
1 cup boiling water

Serves 1

Place the tea leaves in a bowl that has a cover. Add the water and cover. Steep for 3 to 4 minutes. When it's time to drink the tea, the cover can be used to push the tea leaves aside, or, alternatively, the cover can be shifted only slightly off-center so that it holds back the tea leaves during drinking.

THE YIXING TEAPOT

The covered bowl method can be used for any tea being prepared for one person. The Yixing teapot is ideal for preparing tea for a group of people. The tight-fitting lids of these teapots hold the steam well and, with the natural insulating qualities of the clay, the pot holds the water's heat during the entire steeping process.

When the methods for brewing tea turned away from the powdered and whisked methods and began to use the whole leaf, the need for new vessels also arose. Most experts agree that the lid, handle, and spout of the teapot were modeled on wine ewers.

Yixing teapots are named after a county situated to the west of the beautiful Lake Taihu in the Jiangsu province of China. In the early sixteenth century, a Buddhist monk from the Golden Sand Temple, located southeast of Yixing, appeared in the village one day calling out, "Riches and honor for sale!" The villagers jeered him. Unperturbed, he said, "If you do not care for honors, how about riches?" He then led the people to a cave containing clays of different and brilliant colors. This same nameless monk is said to have made his own teapots, each one marked with his own thumbprint.

Some time later, a scholar named Wu Yishan came to picturesque Yixing to study for his civil examination. His young servant, Gongchun, met the monk from the Golden Sand Temple and began making teapots while his master was studying. Gongchun became famous in his own right, and his designs were copied throughout the centuries. Although we have no authenticated example, an oft-copied design in the shape of a ginkgo tree burl represents his most rustic work. His more refined work, a six-lobed teapot with his signature and a date of 1513, survives to this day and attests to Gongchun's skills.

Eventually, the Yixing teapot was adopted by generations of literati, spiritual masters, and artists. There have been a seemingly endless number of unusual, even eccentric teapots. Some are quite eccentric, imitating pine trunks, pieces of bamboo, wrapped bundles, or a lotus blossom. Others are exquisitely austere, taking their inspiration from a perfect pearl, or even a roof tile.

Yixing teapots have been exported to Europe since the sixteenth century. When large-scale importing of tea began in the mid-seventeenth century, Yixing teapots were imported through private trade. Records show Yixing teapots arriving in England as early as 1620, and Amsterdam in 1680. Eventually, the teapots not only maintained a steady trade to Europe, but came to influence European pottery as well. Dutch, English, and German factories quickly began manufacturing Yixing-inspired teapots and tea paraphernalia.

The Yixing teapot not only excels at maintaining the temperature of the tea, it subtly absorbs the flavor of tea as well. A well-seasoned teapot can have plain hot water poured into it and still impart the flavor of fine tea! That is why a Yixing teapot is never washed with soap and water. To do so is to ruin a beautiful pot. Simply rinse the teapot well, and leave upside down to dry.

When looking for a teapot of your own, make sure that the lid fits tightly, that the body will ring when struck lightly, and that the spout does not drip after you have poured your tea. Look at the teapot from above and make sure that the axes of the spout, center of the lid, and handle all form a straight line. Before using the teapot, place it upside down on a rack over boiling water for an hour to steam it. This drives out any minerals left from the firing process. Fastidious people then submerge their pots in tea—and only in the type of tea which they intend for their new pot—for a few hours each day over an entire week, brewing fresh tea for each soaking. The strictest people reserve a separate pot for each type and grade of tea they favor.

Yixing teapots come in many sizes but the average pot holds enough tea for one person. Some tea drinkers drink directly from the spout, so that none of the tea or its aroma is lost, but the majority of people pour their tea into cups.

Brewing tea in a Yixing teapot is easy. Put 2 to 3 teaspoons of tea leaves into the pot and add hot water. Cover and steep for about 3 to 4 minutes. Never let tea stand for long periods of time in the teapot.

If it is well looked after, a Yixing teapot will last many lifetimes, imparting more and more flavor each time it is used.

GONGFU TEA⌄

The gongfu (skilled) method of brewing tea lends itself best to high-quality oolong and black teas. The equipment needed is elaborate and requires long hours of study. The following description will help you explore this way of making tea, but remember that it is only an introduction.

You will need a small Yixing teapot, a number of small cups, a "tea boat" (a flat vessel with a perforated top upon which the teapot and cups are served), a small wooden tray or dish to hold the tea leaves before serving, a small supplementary porcelain pitcher, a towel, a long bamboo spoon, and a spouted kettle that will keep the water at a constant temperature. (The earliest methods required a servant to fan a flame; modern methods use an electric kettle.)

Serves 4

A small teapot ¼ to ½ full of tea leaves, or about 4 teaspoons
Boiling water

Place the teapot and cups on the tea boat. Pour hot water into the teapot to warm and rinse it. After waiting about 10 to 30 seconds, pour the water liberally over all the cups to heat and rinse them. Keep pouring, even past the point of overflowing, until the teapot is emptied. Then empty the cups into the boat.

Place the tea leaves on a wooden tray. Pass it around for your guests to appreciate the quality of the leaves and to savor the fragrance of the tea.

The long bamboo tea spoon has a flat spade shape at one end, and tapers to a long point at the other. The point is used to clear the spout and body of the teapot. The flat end is used to gently fill the teapot with the tea leaves. A great deal of tea is used in this method of brewing.

Pour a few drops of hot water into the tea. Wait a few seconds, and then allow your guests to smell the emerging bouquet.

Fill the teapot with boiling water and cover. Let steep for about 3 to 4 minutes. During this and other waiting times, use the moments for quiet contemplation, appreciation of the tea ware, art objects, or natural scenery, or gracious discourse. You can serve various snacks during this time, as much as suits your fancy. The snacks can be as simple as a plate of fresh green soybeans or fava beans, to elaborate sweets and, of course, dim sum dumplings.

If the teapot will make enough tea to fill all the cups, group the cups so they are touching, and pour the tea by moving the spout constantly and repeatedly over all the cups so that all cups have the same strength of tea. With the tea boat to catch the drainage, you need not worry about spilling. It is more important to maintain a steady stream from the spout until the teapot is emptied.

If there is more tea than will go into the cups, pour the excess into the porcelain pitcher, so the tea will not continue to steep and become bitter. Some people like to pour all the contents of the teapot into the pitcher first, so that steeping is halted immediately.

Serve your friends, from left to right. Pick up each cup, and lightly touch it to a towel, which should be folded neatly on the table before you, and then present the cup. Always serve with both hands, as a sign of respect. Intimate friends simply take their own cups from the tea boat.

You can either sip the tea, or drink it in one gulp. When each person is done, he or she places the cup back on the tea boat.

When everyone has finished, repeat the steeping and pouring. Very good grades of tea should last through at least three pourings, and sometimes as many as eight.

THE CHANOYU BOWL

THE BOWL

We rarely eat without a bowl on our table. The bowl is fundamental, and it is also a great spiritual symbol.

When Siddarta first left the palace on the journey that would lead to his enlightenment, he took only a robe and bowl.

Buddhist precepts speak of the pleasures of having a single robe that no one would want to steal, a simple clay bowl, and the shade of a tree.

When the Fifth Master made Huineng his successor, he did so by presenting him with a robe and a bowl.

In the Taoist White Cloud Temple in Beijing, the bowl of its founder, made from the single burl of a tree and with its edge gilded by imperial order, has survived centuries of warfare, including the Cultural Revolution, and it is still enshrined there.

When the spiritual practice of tea first came to Japan, it brought with it precious tea bowls with such glazes as the Oil Spot glaze and the Rabbit's Fur glaze. When masters like Rikyu wanted to revolutionize tea-drinking, they championed the making of local, handmade raku bowls. Both types of bowls are still revered today, and the best bowls throughout the centuries are carefully treasured in Zen temples.

The Taoists ask you this: What is the usefulness of a bowl? Isn't it in the emptiness?

So your bowl, that apparently most utilitarian of objects, has a long history, and the potential for imparting spiritual history and spiritual knowledge as well.

Chanoyu means the hot water used for tea. While it is often translated as the tea ceremony or tea ritual, chanoyu is neither ritual nor ceremony. Rather, chanoyu is a gathering where host and guests set aside daily concerns, to focus on food, art, nature, and conversation over a shared bowl of tea. For the individual, chanoyu is an opportunity to forget one's daily self in the practice of drinking tea, which thus becomes a means of spiritual contemplation within the purity of that moment.

Based on the idea that elaborate etiquette can actually be liberating, chanoyu has evolved into a structured event. Throughout the different styles of chanoyu (from imperial to casual), the actions of the host and the guests are rigorously formalized. The gestures, forms of speech, and patterns of movement may seem arbitrary and restrictive to outsiders, but they actually free the host to express greater hospitality and allow the guests to respond without worry.

With every action, word, and gesture clearly understood and well rehearsed, each of the participants instead concentrates on the event itself. They become aware of the unique, unrepeatable quality of the moment, as expressed in the phrase, ichigo ichie—one (meaning singular and unique) moment (meaning a definite and limited period of time), one meeting (meaning joining, culmination, association, and opportunity).

The phrase ichigo ichie is a reminder of Ii Naosuke (1815–1860), a tea master and chief administrator for the Tokugawa Shogunate who instituted many radical social changes. His many enemies constantly threatened him with assassination. Before he left his home for his duties each morning, he sat alone and made himself a bowl of tea, saying that it was a unique and unrepeatable tea—ichigo ichie. In spite of the constant danger, he would drink and meditate upon his tea. Ii Naosuke was assassinated on a snowy morning, but his words became the most important motto for Zen tea students.

THE HISTORY OF POWDERED GREEN TEA IN JAPAN

When Zen master Eisai (1192–1219) traveled to China, he brought tea and tea seeds back to Japan. When he served tea, Eisai seated his guests around the perimeters of the temple hall. A monk presented each guest with a Chinese tea bowl containing a small amount of powdered green tea, and set it on a lacquer stand. Each guest held his bowl in both hands while a second monk added hot water and whisked the tea.

The aristocracy, warriors, and merchants subsequently incorporated tea into lavish banquets and drinking parties, and abandoned the austerity of the Zen temples. They built pavilions imitating a Zen abbot's quarters—but with much more opulent materials—and filled them with priceless collections of Chinese art. They also used precious utensils for serving tea.

When the Ashikaga shogunate collapsed in the sixteenth century, Japan entered a hundred-year period of civil war. Influenced by Zen philosophy, tea masters brought tea back to its more serene spiritual practice. It is during this age that chanoyu as it is known today was created.

The sixteenth-century tea master and Zen practitioner, Sen Rikyu (1522–1591), took the elaborate aristocratic forms of chanoyu and combined them with the more subtle forms influenced by Zen. He brought the spirit of art and philosophy, and the ideals of Zen Buddhism, to the serving of tea and food. Pruning away many of the excesses of consumption, as well as championing rustic and native implements to counter the mania for opulent Chinese art, Rikyu formulated the ideals of chanoyu. These four principles, introduced at the beginning of this book, inspire Zen cooking and chanoyu even to this day: harmony (wa), respect (kei), purity (sei), and tranquillity (jaku).

For the past four hundred years, the philosophy and spirit of chanoyu, as created by Sen Rikyu, have continued to be a vital aspect of Japanese culture. Dr. Sen Soshitsu XV, present head of the Urasenke Tradition of Chanoyu and fifteenth-generation descendant of Sen Rikyu, has spent his lifetime promoting the Way of Tea in Japan and abroad. Dr. Sen firmly believes that the philosophy and aesthetics of tea can be fully understood by everybody, and that a new world of peace may come from the simple act of sharing a bowl of tea.

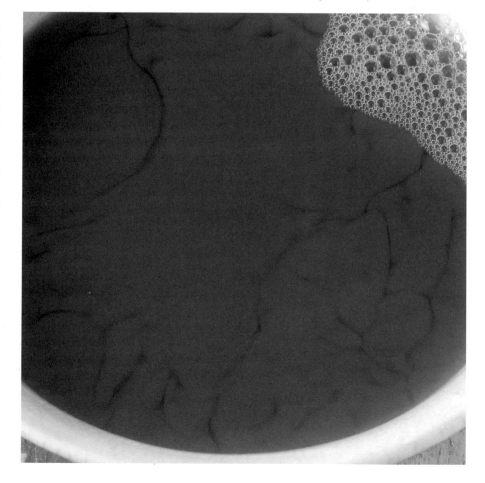

POWDERED GREEN TEA

The leaves for powdered green tea—matcha—are hand-picked in Japan during the month of May when the first new growth has appeared. Only the first three to five young leaves from each stem are used for matcha; the remainder goes to lesser teas and other uses. After harvesting, the leaves are steamed to preserve their bright green color, to keep their fresh taste, and to slow further oxidation. Differing microclimates, soil conditions, and the age of the tea plant produce tea leaves with different colors, flavors, and aromas. Experts take leaves from different varietals and plantations to make highly-regarded blends, ranging in taste from bitter and toasted to light and sweet.

The tea is then packed into large jars and allowed to age for six months in a cool storehouse. The tea leaves are then slowly ground between millstones.

Two types of matcha are served at a formal tea gathering. First, the host prepares a bowl of thick tea, called koicha. This bowl is shared by the guests—each one turning the bowl so that the next person will have a clean spot on the rim from which to drink.

Koicha is made by slowly blending the finest-quality powdered tea with hot water. The consistency and color of this tea resembles pesto sauce. It requires years of practice to prepare a good bowl of koicha.

After the guests have shared the koicha, the host will prepare individual bowls of thin tea, called usucha. A well-made bowl of usucha is light and frothy, and preparing usucha is one of the first lessons for a tea student.

HOW TO PREPARE A BOWL OF USUCHA⌄

Knowledgeable tea-lovers are familiar with the growing regions for each of their favorite teas. One of the most famous regions in Japan for growing the tea used for matcha is Uji, south of Kyoto. There are many companies, such as Koyamaen, Tsujirien, and Ippodo, that are famous for their excellent matcha. Matcha is usually sold in small tins or foil packets, which are often available in Japanese grocery stores. Like any herb or spice, the flavor of tea quickly diminishes after it has been ground. When you buy matcha, always check the tin or packet to make sure it is the freshest available. Store any unused tea in an airtight container in the freezer.

Tea bowls, tea whisks, and other tea implements are available in Japanese supermarkets.

Serves 1

1/2 to 1 teaspoon matcha
5 fluid ounces water, heated to just below boiling

Warm a Japanese tea bowl or café-au-lait bowl with hot water. Empty and dry the bowl. Place the matcha in the bowl. Add the hot water. Using a bamboo tea whisk, whisk the tea until light and frothy. Drink immediately. The tea should be drunk quickly, in a few sips. If the tea sits too long, the tea powder will settle to the bottom of the bowl and will not taste good.

With practice and experience, you should have no difficulty making a delicious bowl of tea.

KAISEKI

A light meal at a chanoyu gathering is called kaiseki, and is a prelude to the serving of the two types of powdered green tea, matcha and usucha. The word kai refers to the opening formed when one side of a kimono or Zen robe overlaps the other above a tied sash. Seki means stone. Thus, kaiseki means a small warmed stone, which Zen monks placed in their robes to stave off hunger pangs during hours of meditation. Reflecting this austere and frugal custom, a kaiseki meal is simple and unpretentious, and is meant as a prelude to the drinking of tea.

Kaiseki should be composed of many small successive courses, masterful cooking techniques, and the freshest of seasonal ingredients. Originally vegetarian, kaiseki eventually incorporated seafood, poultry, and meats. It still eschews the overly elaborate and the merely ornamental. The genius of its expression is in the careful choice of foods and serving containers. The foods and the containers can be quietly lavish or rustic, but they are always an expression of the host's exquisite and individual taste.

ZEN VERSES

Every tea gathering has a scroll with an inspirational verse. Here is a sampling of Zen verses from the Zenrin Kushu (Zen Forest Verse Collection) *seemingly related to food, along with brief interpretations.*

Mute child savors the taste of honey.
A mute child cannot express the sweet taste of honey; a taste of Zen enlightenment renders a person mute. This is reminiscent of Lao Zi's statement about Tao: "Those who know do not speak. Those who speak do not know."

Oh! I swallowed it!
Meaning swallowing the whole universe.

She chews the food and then feeds it to her baby.
An expression of the many years of training a Zen master instills into a student.

You can't swallow it and you can't spit it out.
The struggle of a Zen-seeker. In seeking yourself, you cannot find yourself, and yet you cannot lose yourself.

A cup of poisoned wine right into your face.
The only way to survive a Zen teacher's instruction is to swallow it in one gulp.

Swallow up the mountain, river, and the great earth.
After you swallow such a huge amount, you will surely burp; just as after you have awakened to Zen, you must surely pass it on.

Not even beautiful food appeals to someone with a full stomach.
People are too filled with distractions to seek Zen. This is like the scholar who went to visit a Zen master. The master poured tea until the cup was full, and then kept pouring. "Enough!" cried the scholar. "The cup is too full!" The master replied: "Until you empty your cup, how is there room for Zen?"

With coarse chewing, you are quickly satisfied. With fine chewing, you are seldom hungry.
One should not hurry through Zen practice.

A person who is eating has neither greed nor anger.
A wonderful way to practice diplomacy.

Turn delusion and passion into enlightenment.
This is the motto of the Zen cook.

A CLASSIC TEA GATHERING

Understanding traditional kaiseki will give you an idea of how much you may want to adapt the theory to your own life. Perhaps you will like the way a tea room can be a powerful retreat from daily stresses. Maybe you will be intrigued by the delicate and sensitive handling of food. Or you may find that you are one of many people who becomes fascinated by tea in all its forms.

A traditional tea ceremony following a kaiseki meal typically includes: an eight-course kaiseki meal; the building of the charcoal fire that heats the water for tea; preparation of one bowl of thick tea that is shared by all the guests; the rebuilding of the fire; and preparation of individual bowls of tea for each guest.

The eight courses are as follows:

FIRST: rice, miso soup, and a side dish (mukozuke, meaning something placed to the far side).
SECOND: food simmered in broth (nimono) or food piled up in a bowl (wanmori).
THIRD AND FOURTH: grilled foods (yakimono), rice, assembled foods (azukebachi), and sake.
FIFTH: palate cleanser (kosuimono).
SIXTH: things from the mountains (yamanomono) and things from the sea (uminomonol), served on a tray (hassun).

SEVENTH: browned rice-crust soup served in a lacquer pitcher (yuto) and dish of pieces (konomono).
EIGHTH: sweets (omogashi).

HOW TO USE THE KAISEKI RECIPES

In planning a tea gathering, the host thoughtfully considers the guests and occasion, and then selects tea utensils and a kaiseki menu that best expresses each unique event. Often at a tea gathering, rustic, seemingly unsophisticated utensils will be paired with elaborately decorated pieces. In kaiseki, too, one finds a contrasting range of flavors and cooking techniques. The dynamic that comes about through such contrast is at the heart of tea harmony.

The host selects foods that are in season and prepares them in a straightforward way. Equal consideration is given to the selection of serving utensils. It is not necessary to have a complete set of kaiseki lacquerware, or even a variety of Japanese ceramics, in order to serve your guests food in the spirit of kaiseki. Think of the color, texture, and amount of food that you are serving and then select dishes that will create a harmonious visual effect.

Instead of presenting these menus in the standard kaiseki way, you may choose to select some of the recipes and arrange the different foods on individual lacquer trays, or even large plates. The nimono can be served as a separate course, either in a standard lidded lacquer bowl or a soup bowl. This simplified form of kaiseki is known as tenshin. The rice served at a tenshin gathering is usually mixed with an additional ingredient, such as green peas for spring. Flavored rice is often pressed into individual shapes and served at room temperature. After the meal, serve tea sweets or fresh fruit, and bowls of tea to your guests.

When arranging the food for tenshin, the rice and pickles are customarily placed on the left side of the tray towards the front, and chopsticks and sake cups are placed on the right. The remaining foods should be placed simply and distinctly in a pleasing arrangement on the tray.

However you decide to use these recipes, as long as you keep in mind the spirit of harmony, respect, purity, and tranquillity, you and your guests will be able to savor the essence of the Way of Tea.

The following recipes are arranged seasonally, to show the way that Zen cooking changes from season to season, and to give a sense of how harmony is achieved through successive courses.

KAISEKI RICE^v

The rice served at a kaiseki meal is short-grain Japanese rice, which is available in supermarkets and Japanese specialty shops. Rice has always been a precious food in Japan. The wealthy ate refined and luxurious polished white rice, while the less wealthy augmented their rice with millet, barley, and other grains. The importance of rice in the Japanese diet is so central that the word for cooked rice (ghana) is synonymous with the word for a meal in general. Just as Zen temple cooks are warned not to let even one grain of rice go to waste, you can use the same scrupulous attention to the preparation of rice in your tearoom or your home.

Rice is served four times during a tea gathering. First each guest is served a small portion of the just-cooked rice in an individual covered bowl. The remainder of the rice continues to cook throughout the meal. The second serving of rice is placed in a round lidded lacquer container, one small but distinct portion per guest. For the third serving, the rice is heaped in the container so that the guests may take as much as they like. The fourth serving is a broth of lightly salted water and the browned rice crust from the bottom of the pot. Along with pickled vegetables, this is the penultimate course of a kaiseki meal. The kaiseki way of serving rice follows the Zen temple practice of using all the rice prepared for a meal, without wasting any, and gives the guests all the tastes and textures of rice in the various stages of cooking.

The freshest rice yields the best food. Always use the current year's crop. When buying rice from a Japanese grocery store, buy in bulk, and make sure the rice grains are whole and not broken.

Serves 4 guests, four times throughout the meal

3 cups Japanese short-grain rice
3 tablespoons dry sake
3³/4 cups cold water
1 teaspoon salt

The rice must be washed first in several changes of cold water to remove the coating of starch applied in its milling. Use your hands to lift the rice from the bottom of the bowl of water to the top. Do not scrub the rice between your hands, as this could break up the grains. Drain the washed rice in a sieve and allow to sit for 30 minutes. The water clinging to the rice will begin to swell the individual grains and will thus help keep them separate when cooked.

Place the rice, sake, water, and salt in a wide, heavy pot. (It does not really matter what kind of pot you use as long as it is heavy enough to conduct heat evenly and has a tight-fitting lid. Also, cooking rice in a pot that is wider than it is deep will help it to cook evenly.) Cover and place over a medium-high heat. Cook for 5 to 10 minutes or until steam begins to escape from the pot.

Turn the heat to medium-low and allow the rice to cook for a further 25 minutes. At about 20 to 25 minutes, the aroma of cooked rice should be very distinct.

HOMEMADE SWEET BEAN PASTE˅

This recipe, using cannellini beans, produces a sweet and mild paste to which food coloring may be added. It may then be used to make sweets of varying colors, depending on the season. Azuki beans can also be prepared in this way, to make a bean paste that is dark brown and rich-tasting. Sweetened bean paste will keep in the freezer for up to 3 months.

Makes approximately 24 tea sweets

1 pound dried cannellini beans, picked over for small stones and damaged beans
1¹⁄₂ cups sugar

Wash the beans in several changes of cold water, then place in a large bowl and cover with cold water. Soak the beans overnight.

Drain the soaked beans and rinse with cold water. Place the beans in a large pan and cover with fresh cold water. Bring to a boil. After the beans have boiled for about 1 minute, drain them and rinse well with cold water. Put the beans back into the pan, cover with fresh cold water, and bring to a boil. Repeat the process of boiling the beans for 1 minute, draining, and rinsing them in cold water two more times. Parboiling the beans in this way produces a very mild-tasting bean paste.

Place the parboiled beans back in the pan and cover with fresh cold water. Bring to a boil, reduce the heat, and simmer for about 1 hour or until the beans are totally soft.

Purée the beans with their cooking liquid in small batches in a blender or food processor. Press the puréed beans through a fine sieve to remove the small bits of skin and germ. At this point you should have a liquid, smooth purée of beans.

Line a colander with a large double layer of cheesecloth. Pour the purée into the colander. Carefully lift the corners of the cheesecloth and wring out all excess liquid. You should be left with a moist purée that resembles mashed potatoes.

Place the purée in a heavy pan and add the sugar. The bean purée will liquefy as the sugar dissolves. Taste for sweetness and adjust the amount of sugar. Bring the purée to a simmer, stirring constantly to prevent scorching. Cook the purée until it resembles very stiff mashed potatoes.

Place a piece of cheesecloth on a wooden cutting board. Turn the paste onto the cloth to cool.

The cooled bean paste may be divided into suitable portions and lightly tinted with food coloring. When coloring the bean paste, always keep in mind the season in which it is to be served. Light shades of pink and green evoke spring; purple and blue suggest summer flowers; scarlet and yellow are reminders of autumn leaves; and pure white symbolizes winter snow.

You will want several colors. Choose one of those colors and make a 1-tablespoon ball for each guest. Using more paste in different colors, press through fine and coarse sieves to create filaments. Use very thin, damp chopsticks to lightly mold the bean paste filaments around each ball.

The sweets will keep in an airtight container overnight. They will lose their taste if prepared any farther in advance.

SERVING SWEETS

Two types of sweets are served at a chanoyu gathering, moist sweets (omogashi) and dry sweets (higashi). The kaiseki meal usually concludes with confections prepared from slightly moist, sweetened bean paste. The flavor is mild. Sweet bean paste confections have the shape and texture of candy truffles.

Dry sweets are served along with individual bowls of thin tea (usucha) during the last part of the tea gathering. Dried sweets are often prepared from refined Japanese sugar, tinted and formed into a variety of seasonal shapes and motifs. The colors, shapes, textures, flavors, and poetic names of tea sweets are always carefully chosen by the host to reflect the season and mood of each chanoyu gathering.

There are many famous tea-sweet shops in Kyoto and throughout Japan. In fact, one of the oldest and most famous confectioners, Toraya, has shops in New York and Paris. Most major cities with a large Japanese population will have a shop where traditional Japanese tea sweets are prepared and sold. However, the best sweets for a chanoyu gathering are handmade by the host. Even if the confections do not have the same polish as those prepared by a sweet shop, the taste and effort come from the heart.

If sweet-bean confections are not to your liking, conclude the kaiseki meal with some fresh or dried seasonal fruit, plain wafers, and the like. In fact, dried fruit and nuts are among the tea sweets mentioned in the diaries of early tea masters.

DOGEN'S RICE

Zen master Dogen opened Japan's first Zen monastery in the thirteenth century. He was born into a time of great upheaval. Not only were there constant power struggles among the nobility and samurai, but there were corresponding conflicts between several Buddhist sects as well. Born an aristocrat and well-tutored in literature, the arts, and the Chinese classics, Dogen turned to the religious life upon the death of his mother. He traveled to China, trained rigorously, and returned to establish the Soto tradition of Zen.

Dogen left behind temples and a large body of well-respected writings. He strongly supported the lay practice of Zen:

"In China, kings and ministers, officials and commoners, men and women all kept to the ancestors' way. Warriors and scholars alike practiced Chan and studied the Tao. Many became enlightened— worldly duties do not hinder the dharma."

It's no surprise that Dogen also paid great attention to cooking. Here is a brief summary of his instructions for cooking rice.

Tie back your sleeves to seek the Tao. Respect the food as though it were for the emperor. Care for all food equally, whether it is raw or cooked. Wash the rice and vegetables with your own hands and be watchful with your own eyes. Make a sincere effort. Don't be idle even for a moment. Don't be careless. Don't lose an opportunity even for one ounce of praise...

Watch for sand when you examine the rice. Watch for rice when you wash away the grit. If you look carefully and remain alert, the three virtues (mildness, cleanliness, and formality) and the six tastes (bitter, sour, sweet, hot, salty, and plain) will be complete.

As an ancient master said, "When you boil rice, know that the water is your own life."

THE KAISEKI WAY OF SERVING RICE

The first serving is taken from the portion of the rice at the top edge. This is the area that cooks the fastest. In the Urasenke tradition of chanoyu, the first serving, sufficient for just three bites, is placed in the rice bowl so that the rice resembles the Japanese character one (ichi, written as a single straight line). To create this shape, use a damp rice paddle, about 3 inches wide, and press down lightly on top of the rice at the edge of the pot. Dampen the paddle again, then cut down at a slight angle, lift off a section of rice, and place it carefully in the bowl.

For the second serving of rice, larger individual portions are scooped and placed in the center of the lacquered rice container. Since the rice is very sticky, you need to be careful not to let any touch the sides of the container, which would smear the lacquer.

For the third serving, the rice is heaped in the container. Again, care should be taken not to let the rice touch the sides.

After the third serving, the pot is placed over a low flame so that the rice clinging to the bottom will toast. This may take about 15 minutes. As the rice forms a brown crust, it will come away from the bottom of the pot.

BROWNED RICE-CRUST SOUP^v

Break the rice crust into small pieces and place them in the lacquered ewer (yuto) or bowl. Add hot water and a large pinch of salt. About 1/2 cup of browned rice-crust and 4 cups hot water makes 4 servings of soup.

A SPRING KAISEKI MENU

First Course
Rice
White Kyoto Miso with Baby Turnips and Mustard
Shrimp with Avocado and Lime

Second Course
Fish Mousse with Shiitake Mushrooms and Broccoli Rabe

Third Course
Grilled Miso-Marinated Tofu

Fourth Course
Asparagus with Lemon

Fifth Course
Light Broth Flavored with Salted Cherry Blossoms

Sixth Course
Sugarsnap Peas and Smoked Salmon

Seventh Course
Lightly Pickled Radish
Vinegared Cucumber
Takuan
Browned Rice-Crust Soup

Eighth Course
Tea Sweets or Fresh Strawberries

WHITE KYOTO MISO WITH BABY TURNIPS AND MUSTARD˅

Baby turnips, simmered with some of their green tops, are one of the delights of early spring. However, any baby vegetable, such as zucchini or even new potatoes, can be substituted for the turnips. If you cannot find white Kyoto miso, regular beige miso could be used. Taste the miso to make sure it is not too strong and salty. Adjust the amount to suit your own taste. Also note the use of a Japanese mortar (suribachi) for grinding the miso. Grinding the miso makes a very smooth and refined miso soup. If you do not have a Japanese mortar, use a blender or food processor. You can also simply blend the miso and dashi together, then strain the mixture.

Soup flavored with miso (fermented soybean paste) is part of everyday cooking in Japan. In kaiseki a small portion of miso soup is one of the first foods the guests are served. The garnish for kaiseki miso soup is usually a seasonal vegetable, simmered in lightly salted water, topped with a dab of mustard. The seasonal ingredient adds interest, while the sharpness of the mustard accentuates the flavors of the soup.

Serves 4

5 tablespoons white Kyoto miso
3 cups Basic Dashi or Shiitake Dashi
(see page 33)
4 baby turnips, each about 2 inches in diameter, with green tops
1 tablespoon Japanese short-grain rice
2 teaspoons yellow mustard powder
(English, Chinese, or Japanese)

Place the miso in a Japanese mortar (suribachi) and grind until smooth. While grinding, gradually add the dashi.

Pass the miso through a fine sieve. Discard the solids, and strain the miso soup two more times. (It can be set aside for several hours at room temperature, then heated just before serving.)

Wash the turnips. Make sure that there is no soil clinging to the base of the stems. Trim the stems, leaving about 1 inch. If the turnips are large you may want to cut them in half.

Place the turnips in a pan with the raw rice and cover with cold water. (Cooking the turnips with a little rice softens their sometimes sharp flavor.) Bring the water to a simmer and cook until just done, about 15 minutes. Remember that the turnips will be eaten with chopsticks and so should be cooked until soft, but not falling apart.

Dissolve the mustard powder in enough hot water to form a thick paste. Cover and let sit for at least 10 minutes to deepen the flavor. Thin the mustard paste with 1/2 cup of the soup.

To serve, bring the miso soup to a simmer. Do not let it boil as this will make it taste very harsh. Divide the turnips among 4 lacquered soup bowls with lids. Carefully ladle in the hot soup until most but not all of the turnip is submerged. Place a drop of mustard on the turnip, cover the bowl with the lid, and then serve.

SHRIMP WITH AVOCADO AND LIME

This spring mukozuke (something placed to the far side) is meant to be just a few bites of food pleasingly arranged on individual serving dishes.

Serves 4

12 raw medium shrimp or large prawns, in shell
1 ripe avocado
2 limes
4 tablespoons light soy sauce

Rinse the shrimp. Skewer each one lengthwise on a bamboo or small wooden skewer. (This will keep them from curling when cooked.)

Half fill a saucepan with water. Salt the water to taste. Bring the water to a boil, then cook the shrimp until they turn pink and opaque, approximately 3 to 5 minutes. Remove the shrimp and chill in ice water. Afterwards, remove the skewers and peel the shrimp. Butterfly each shrimp and refrigerate.

Peel the avocado and cut into bite-size pieces. Toss with the juice of one of the limes to prevent discoloration.

Grate the zest from the remaining lime and juice it. Mix the lime juice with the soy sauce and set aside.

Toss the shrimp with the avocado. Spoon the lime and soy dressing on the bottom of the serving dishes and carefully mound the shrimp and avocado on top. Sprinkle with the grated lime zest and serve.

FISH MOUSSE WITH SHIITAKE MUSHROOMS AND BROCCOLI RABE

Fish mousse (shinjo) is a versatile classic of kaiseki cuisine. It can be prepared with any type of fine white fish or shrimp. Shinjo is heavier than Western-style fish mousse, making it easier to eat with chopsticks. It may be steamed in a large pan and cut into decorative shapes, or prepared in individual molds. Use only the freshest fish.

The richness of the shiitake mushrooms and the slight bitterness of the broccoli rabe lend contrast in this dish, while the seasoned broth ties the flavors together. The garnish of lemon peel adds a wonderful fragrance that is especially noticeable just as the lids are removed from the bowls.

You will need 4 molds of 1/2-cup capacity, or a square pan of 2-cup capacity, lightly oiled.

Serves 4

FOR THE SEASONED BROTH	**FOR THE FISH MOUSSE**	**THE SECONDARY INGREDIENTS**
3 cups Basic Dashi *(see page 33)*	12 ounces white fish fillets, such as sole, cod, or sea bass	4 medium dried shiitake mushrooms or black mushrooms
2 tablespoons light soy sauce	1 egg white	1 lemon
4 tablespoons sake	1/2 teaspoon salt	A seasoning of sake, soy sauce, and sugar
A pinch of salt	2 tablespoons sake	1 small bunch broccoli rabe
A large pinch of sugar	3/4 cup cold Basic Dashi *(see page 33)*	

Bring the dashi to a simmer and add the other ingredients. Taste the broth and adjust the seasonings. (The seasoned broth may be removed from the heat and set aside for up to 1 hour.)

To prepare the fish mousse, wash the fish fillets in cold water and pat dry with paper towels. Cut the fish into medium pieces. Place the fish in a food processor and process until smooth. Add the egg white and process until it is incorporated. Add the salt and sake. Gradually add the cold dashi.

Place the mousse in the lightly oiled molds or pan. (The prepared mousse may be covered tightly with plastic wrap and kept in the refrigerator for up to 30 minutes.)

Rinse the dried shiitake mushrooms and soak in 2 cups of water until rehydrated. Remove the stems and place the mushrooms and the soaking liquid in a small pan. Season to taste with sake, soy sauce, and a pinch of sugar. Gently simmer the seasoned mushrooms for 15 minutes, then remove from the heat and let sit until needed.

Wash the broccoli rabe. Select four of the best-formed flowering stalks and cut them into 3-inch lengths. Bring some lightly salted water to a boil and parboil the broccoli rabe until the hearts of the stem just turn translucent. The rabe may be kept warm in a little hot dashi.

Using a vegetable peeler, remove four strips of peel from the lemon. Trim each strip to be 2 inches long and 1/4 inch wide.

When ready to cook the fish mousse, line the interior and lid of a large steamer with cheesecloth or muslin. This will prevent steam from condensing and dropping onto the mousse. Bring water in the steamer to a boil. Place the molds or pan of fish mousse into the steamer. Cover and steam for 15 to 20 minutes. Test by inserting a toothpick into the center of the mousse. If the center is cooked and the mousse is firm, it is done.

Unmold the mousse. If you cooked it in a large pan, carefully turn it out onto a clean cutting board and cut into servings—squares, diamonds, or whatever shape suits your fancy. However, you want to keep in mind the size of the bowl in which it will be served.

Place one serving of mousse to the rear of each bowl. Stand a mushroom against the left front of the mousse. Place the broccoli rabe with the stem to the front right and the flower on top of the mousse. Carefully ladle 3/4 cup of seasoned broth into each of the bowls. Place the lemon peel on top of the mousse. Cover the bowls and serve immediately.

GRILLED MISO-MARINATED TOFU^v

Although this dish uses only a few ingredients, the smoky flavor is just the right way to follow up the previous dish. Be sure to start the recipe two days before you plan to serve it.

Serves 4

14 ounces firm tofu
1½ cups white Kyoto miso
½ cup sake

Rinse the tofu, then place in a pan and cover with cold water. Bring to a boil and remove from the heat. Drain the tofu and wrap in cheesecloth or muslin. Place the tofu on a cutting board and place another cutting board on top. Put a 2-pound weight on top of the cutting board (stones or cans of food work well) and press the tofu for 20 minutes to remove excess water.

Whisk the miso and sake together. Spread a layer of this miso mixture on the bottom of a glass or other nonreactive container. Remove the pressed tofu from the cheesecloth and place on top of the miso mixture. Evenly cover the sides and top of the tofu with the remaining miso mixture. Cover and refrigerate for 2 days.

When you are ready to cook, pour off most of the miso mixture from the tofu. Slice the tofu into four pieces.

Grill the tofu under the broiler until the top is golden, approximately 8 to 10 minutes. Place on a warmed serving dish and serve immediately.

ASPARAGUS WITH LEMON^v

Meyer lemons are sweeter and more fragrant than other varieties of lemons. If they are not available, ordinary lemons may be substituted and the quantity of juice reduced to taste.

Serves 4

12 asparagus spears, woody ends removed

FOR THE DRESSING
3 egg yolks
1 teaspoon sugar
¼ teaspoon salt
¾ cup cold water
1 tablespoon cornstarch .
3 tablespoons Meyer lemon juice
1 teaspoon finely grated Meyer lemon zest

Cut the asparagus into even pieces about 2 inches long. Parboil the asparagus in lightly salted water until just cooked—the outside should be bright green and the hearts should be barely translucent. Drain and plunge into cold water. Place the asparagus on paper towels to dry while you prepare the dressing.

Place the egg yolks, sugar, salt, cold water, cornstarch, and 2 tablespoons of the lemon juice in the top of a double boiler and whisk together. Cook over simmering water, whisking constantly, until the mixture thickens, approximately 5 to 6 minutes. Pour the dressing into a bowl and allow to cool. Taste and add the remaining lemon juice if necessary. Mix in the grated lemon zest.

Place the asparagus in a neat pile in a serving bowl and top with some of the dressing.

LIGHT BROTH FLAVORED WITH SALTED CHERRY BLOSSOMS^v

Hashiarai literally means "chopstick rinse." It follows the main courses of the kaiseki meal and, like sorbet, refreshes the palate. The standard base for the hashiarai is hot water, subtly flavored with dried kelp. Salted cherry blossoms are available in most well-stocked Japanese grocery stores; any herb blossom, such as clusters of thyme or single sage blossoms, may be used as a substitute.

Hashiarai is served in small lidded lacquer cups. The lids are used to hold the foods that will be served in the hassun course *(see page 132).*

Serves 4

4 salted cherry blossoms
1 cup water
1 piece konbu (dried kelp),
approximately 2 x 5 inches

Place one blossom in each serving cup.

Bring the water to a boil. Add the konbu and remove from the heat. Leave the kelp in the hot water for 1 minute and then remove. The flavor should be very subtle.

Pour 4 tablespoons of the flavored hot water into each cup, cover, and serve.

LIGHTLY PICKLED RADISH, VINEGARED CUCUMBER, AND TAKUAN WITH BROWNED RICE-CRUST SOUP^ˇ

Kaiseki concludes with a course of pickled vegetables and browned rice-crust broth. For this menu, lightly salted radish and sweet vinegared cucumbers are served with a pungent white radish pickle called takuan. Ever since the Zen priest Takuan introduced this pickle into the Japanese diet in the seventeenth century, it has been a popular food in homes throughout the country.

Takuan is prepared with daikon radish (also called mooli), which is first sun-dried and then pickled in rice bran for several months. There are many wonderful varieties available in Japanese markets. When shopping, look for takuan without artificial colors or preservatives. Takuan will keep for up to a month after opening if stored, well wrapped, in the refrigerator.

Serves 4

8 pieces takuan

FOR THE LIGHTLY PICKLED RADISH
1 bunch (about 8 to 10) red radishes or
6 ounces daikon radish
1 tablespoon seasalt

FOR THE VINEGARED CUCUMBERS
2 Japanese cucumbers or 1 English cucumber (about 6 ounces)
1 tablespoon seasalt
2 tablespoons sugar
4 tablespoons rice vinegar

To prepare the pickled radish, wash the radishes and trim off the tops and root ends. Peel the daikon, then slice both into paper-thin slices. Place in a glass or other nonreactive bowl and toss with the salt. Let sit for about 10 minutes. The radish slices should become limp but still remain crisp. Put the radish pickle in a sieve and rinse with cold water to remove excess salt.

To prepare the cucumbers, wash them and trim off both ends. Cut the cucumbers into 1/4-inch-thick slices. Place them in a glass bowl and sprinkle with the salt. Let the cucumbers sit for about 10 minutes.

Add the sugar to the vinegar and stir until dissolved. Rinse the salted cucumbers and pat them dry with paper towels. Toss them with the sweetened vinegar. Cover and let sit for at least 1 hour. Drain the pickles before serving.

To serve takuan in the kaiseki manner, rinse it well and cut into pieces 1/4 inch thick. Trim these pieces into rectangular shapes. Two rectangles make one serving.

Place the lightly pickled radish, vinegared cucumber, and takuan in distinct mounds on a serving dish. Serve with Browned Rice-Crust Soup (see page 126).

SUGARSNAP PEAS AND SMOKED SALMON

The hassun course is an opportunity for the host and guests to share food and sake. It takes its name from the square cedarwood tray on which the food is placed. The foods for this course are poetically described as coming from the mountains and the seas, and should be of contrasting flavors and appearances. Smoked, salted, or other forms of prepared fish are classic choices for the hassun course. Whatever foods you choose to serve, they should be arranged on the tray with the food from the mountains on the upper right and the food from the seas on the lower left. For a tea gathering the amount of food is set so that there is one serving of each food for the host and guests and one serving left over to signify generosity.

Any smoked fish, or even prosciutto, can be used as a substitute for the smoked salmon.

Serves 4

8 sugarsnap peas
8 slices smoked salmon
8 capers (optional)

Parboil the sugarsnap peas in lightly salted water until bright green. Plunge immediately into cold water.

Roll the smoked salmon into bundles. Alternatively, place a caper on each slice of smoked salmon and fold it in half.

Arrange the pea pods in a neat pile on the upper right and the salmon on the lower left of a lightly dampened hassun tray.

A SUMMER KAISEKI MENU

First Course
Rice
Summer Miso Soup
Tomatoes, Shaved Celery, and Arugula with Lemon Soy Sauce

Second Course
Savory Egg Custard with Almonds, Green Beans, and Orange Peel

Third Course
Grilled Portobello Mushrooms

Fourth Course
Wilted Spinach with Pine-Nut Dressing

Fifth Course
Light Broth Flavored with Pickled Plums

Sixth Course
Deep-Fried Konbu and Okra

Seventh Course
Eggplant Pickle
Narazuke
Takuan
Browned Rice-Crust Soup

Eighth Course
Tea Sweets or Fresh Melon

SUMMER MISO SOUP^v

This is a blend of dark red and white miso with zucchini and mustard. As mentioned in the spring miso soup recipe, kaiseki miso soup is always complemented with a seasonal ingredient, usually a simmered vegetable, and mustard. The simple taste of zucchini is a perfect foil for the rich and salty taste of red miso. Red miso varies in strength and degree of saltiness. The amounts given in this recipe should serve only as a guide—before preparing this soup, taste the red miso to determine how much white miso to add. The final result should be rich and deep-flavored, but not overwhelming.

Serves 4

5 tablespoons red miso
1 to 2 tablespoons white miso
3 cups Shiitake Dashi (see page 33)
1 medium zucchini
2 teaspoons powdered yellow mustard
(English, Chinese, or Japanese)

Grind the misos in a Japanese mortar (suribachi), or a blender or food processor, until smooth. Gradually add the shiitake dashi, reserving 2 to 3 tablespoons dashi for thinning the mustard. Pass the miso through a fine-mesh sieve several times, discarding the solids. The miso soup may now be set aside for up to an hour.

Wash and trim the zucchini. Cut it into four 2-inch pieces. Parboil in lightly salted water until just cooked.

Dissolve the mustard in enough hot water to form a thick paste. Cover and let it sit for 10 minutes to develop its flavor. Thin the mustard with the reserved shiitake dashi.

Bring the miso soup to a simmer. Do not boil.

Place one piece of zucchini in each bowl. Carefully ladle the hot miso soup into the bowls. The soup should not completely cover the zucchini. Place a drop of mustard on top of the zucchini, cover the bowls, and serve.

A ZEN PICKLE

Takuan Soho (1573–1645) was born into a samurai family, and he maintained an intimate association with swordsmen—he became a counselor to a kendo (Japanese sword) master, teacher of an emperor, and advisor to a shogun. He is famous for two great essays on Zen and swordsmanship. Among his many accomplishments were a study of the Yi Jing, Confucian scholarship, calligraphy, painting, garden design, and the art of tea. He is credited with the creation of a pickle that still bears the name Takuan in his honor.

So much of cooking depends on slicing, and pickles are no exception. What keeps a dish of pickles from being mere salted vegetables on a plate? It is the way they are sliced. Veteran cooks care as much for good knives as a warrior cares for a good blade. If you doubt that cutting makes that much of a difference, ask yourself how a good sushi chef could possibly present his food beautifully without a good, sharp knife.

You cannot be timid with a knife. You must cut, and cut completely. Try to cut in little strokes and you only make a mess of things. Try to think as you cut, and you only make things worse. When you cut, just cut.

Takuan wrote several famous treatises on the art of the sword. In one, the Annals of the Sword Taia, he discussed a legendary Chinese sword called Taia. It was reputed to be a jeweled sword that could cut anything from steel to stone. No other weapon under heaven could parry it, and Takuan asserted that the person who wielded such a sword could not be opposed even by a commander with hundreds of thousands of men. Such was the mysterious power and sharpness of Taia.

But his writing then takes a surprising turn, and brings the discussion directly to the point of Buddhism: "All people, without exception," wrote Takuan, "possess Taia. In each person, this sword is perfect and complete." Taia, of course, is a metaphor for the mind—the mind which is not born with your birth, the mind that does not die with your death.

TOMATOES, SHAVED CELERY, AND ARUGULA WITH LEMON SOY SAUCE ᵛ

Tomatoes are the quintessential summer vegetable. Paired with arugula and celery, tomatoes make a playful, nontraditional addition to a summer kaiseki.

Serves 4

2 large, vine-ripened tomatoes, peeled
Salt to taste
1 pale green stalk celery
4 tablespoons dark soy sauce
2 tablespoons fresh lemon juice
1 small bunch arugula, or other sharp-tasting green such as watercress

Cut each tomato into eight wedges, taking care to remove the seeds. Lightly salt the tomato wedges.

Using a mandoline, Japanese vegetable slicer, or food processor, shave the celery into paper-thin pieces.

Mix the dark soy sauce with the lemon juice.

When you are ready to present the dish, lightly mound four tomato wedges on each serving dish. Top the tomatoes with the shaved celery and garnish with a few leaves of arugula. Carefully pour the dressing onto the bottom of the dish and serve.

SAVORY EGG CUSTARD WITH ALMONDS, GREEN BEANS, AND ORANGE PEEL ᵛ

This is a variation on the standard savory egg custard often served in kaiseki. The custard may be steamed in small molds or in a large bowl from which individual portions can be scooped. Steam over a low heat, and check several times to avoid overcooking.

Serves 4

FOR THE CUSTARD
3 eggs
1 cup cold Shiitake Dashi (see page 33)
1/4 teaspoon salt
1/2 cup slivered almonds, toasted

THE SECONDARY INGREDIENTS
12 green beans
4 strips orange peel, each 3 inches long

FOR THE SEASONED BROTH
3 cups Shiitake Dashi (see page 33)
Dark soy sauce
Sake
Salt

Beat the eggs lightly together, and add the cold shiitake dashi and salt. Strain through a fine-mesh sieve. Pour the custard into a heatproof bowl or 4 small molds and distribute the almonds over the top. Steam the custard in a cloth-lined steamer over medium-low heat for approximately 20 to 25 minutes. When done, the custard should be firm in the center.

Parboil the beans and trim into lengths suitable for the bowl you're using. Tie each strip of peel into a loose knot.

To prepare the seasoned broth, bring the shiitake dashi to a simmer and season lightly with soy sauce, sake, and salt to taste.

Using a large spoon, carefully scoop individual portions of the custard (or unmold the individual custards) and place in the bowls. Lean three green beans to the side of the custard. Ladle the hot seasoned broth into the bowls. Place an orange peel knot on top of the custard, cover the bowls, and serve.

GRILLED PORTOBELLO MUSHROOMS^v

Grilled mushrooms provide a dark, rich note in an otherwise light vegetarian kaiseki. Portobello mushrooms work best for this recipe, although any large, open-cap cultivated mushroom can be substituted. The mushrooms can also be cooked under the broiler with equally delicious results.

Serves 4

1/2 cup dark soy sauce
1/2 cup sake
4 portobello mushrooms, each about
3 inches in diameter
Salt
Powdered sansho pepper or black pepper

Mix the soy sauce and sake together. Remove the stems from the mushrooms, and marinate the caps in the soy and sake mixture for 15 minutes.

Prepare the charcoal fire and lightly oil the rack with vegetable oil. If cooking under the broiler, lightly oil the pan, which must be very clean. Drain the mushrooms and salt lightly, then grill for 3 to 5 minutes on each side. Cut the mushrooms in half, top with a light dusting of sansho or freshly ground pepper, and serve.

LIGHT BROTH FLAVORED WITH PICKLED PLUMS^v

Small pickled plums (ko umeboshi) packed in brine work best for this recipe.

Serves 4

4 pickled plums, pits removed
1 cup water
1 piece konbu (dried kelp),
approximately 2 x 5 inches

Place one plum in each serving cup.

Bring the water to a boil and remove from the heat. Put the dried kelp in the hot water and steep for about 1 minute, then remove it. Remember, the flavor should be subtle.

Divide the flavored hot water among the four cups, cover, and serve.

WILTED SPINACH WITH PINE-NUT DRESSING^v

Here's an interesting recipe that utilizes a sushi rolling mat to shape an excellent vegetarian dish.

Serves 4

1 pound fresh spinach
1/2 cup pine nuts
2 tablespoons dark soy sauce

Trim the roots but leave the stems on the spinach. Carefully wash in several changes of cold water. Bring a large pan of water to a boil. Add the spinach. Let the water return to a boil, then cook the spinach for 30 seconds or until bright green. Do not overcook. Quickly remove the spinach to a bowl of ice water. When cool, drain the spinach thoroughly.

Place the drained spinach down the length of a bamboo sushi rolling mat, roll up, and gently squeeze dry. If you don't have a sushi rolling mat, a clean dish towel can be used. Unroll the sushi mat or towel, keeping the spinach in a log shape. Cut the spinach log into 2-inch lengths.

Lightly toast the pine nuts. A nonstick frying pan works well for this. Coarsely grind them in a Japanese mortar (suribachi) or coffee grinder. Add the soy sauce. If the dressing is too thick, thin it with some shiitake dashi (see page 33).

Toss the spinach with the dressing until well coated. Lightly heap the spinach in a serving bowl and serve.

DEEP-FRIED KONBU AND OKRA˅

Deep-fried konbu is a traditional component of Zen temple cuisine. Here it is combined with parboiled okra and served as the hassun course. If you are not planning to serve this as a hassun, you can increase the amount of both konbu and okra to suit the occasion.

Serves 4

**6 rectangles of konbu (*dried kelp*),
each 1 x 2 inches
6 small okra
3 cups vegetable oil**

Do not rinse or soak the konbu.

Wash the okra. Trim the stem end, but do not remove the cap. Parboil in lightly salted water until bright green and still crisp. Rinse in cold water and drain.

Bring the oil to medium-high heat. Deep-fry the konbu for about 10 seconds. It will turn from green to light brown and puff slightly when done. Do not overcook or the konbu will taste bitter. Drain on paper towels.

Place the okra in a pile on the upper right of a lightly dampened hassun tray or other dish. Stack the deep-fried konbu on the lower left of the tray and serve immediately.

EGGPLANT PICKLE, NARAZUKE, AND TAKUAN WITH BROWNED RICE-CRUST SOUP˅

Lightly salted vegetables, seasoned with soy sauce, are a typical home-style pickle. Japanese eggplants are at their best and most abundant in the summer, and are ideal for this type of pickle. The amount of pickles you serve depends on your own preference. There are no fixed rules, other than for how takuan are cut and served. Pickles, rice, and miso soup make a frugal, yet delicious meal, very much like those served in Zen temples.

Narazuke is a wonderfully sweet and fragrant pickle. It is made by submerging salted melon in a mixture of sake sediment, sugar, and sweet sake for at least a year. Like takuan, narazuke is usually not made at home, but rather purchased from a specialty shop or market. Narazuke is sold with some of the pickling mixture clinging to it, which should be rinsed off before the pickle is sliced.

Serves 4

**8 pieces takuan
8 pieces narazuke**

**FOR THE EGGPLANT PICKLE
2 medium Japanese eggplants
Salt
Soy sauce**

To make the eggplant pickle, wash the eggplants, remove the stem cap, and cut in half lengthwise. Cut each half into 1-inch pieces. Toss the eggplant with about 3 tablespoons salt and let sit for 15 minutes. Rinse the salted eggplant, place in a dish or tea towel, and squeeze dry. Season the eggplant with 1 to 2 tablespoons soy sauce before serving.

Rinse the takuan and cut into pieces 1/4 inch thick. Trim these pieces into rectangular shapes. Two rectangles make one serving. Rinse the narazuke and slice into bite-size pieces.

Place the eggplant pickle, narazuke, and takuan in distinct mounds on a serving dish. Serve the pickles with Browned Rice-Crust Soup (see page 126).

AN AUTUMN KAISEKI MENU

First Course
Rice
Autumn Miso Soup with Sweet Potato
Crab with White Radish Sprouts

Second Course
Tatsuta Tofu, Chanterelles, Spinach, and Lemon Peel

Third Course
Baked Trout with Sea Urchin Glaze

Fourth Course
Muscat Grapes with Yellow Chrysanthemum Petals

Fifth Course
Light Broth Flavored with Walnuts

Sixth Course
Chestnut Balls and Grilled Peppers

Seventh Course
Green Tomato-Miso Pickles
Vinegared Cucumber
Takuan
Browned Rice-Crust Soup

Eighth Course
Tea Sweets or Persimmons

MELONS TO ENTICE A RECLUSE

Daito Kokushi (1282–1334) was the founder of the largest and most prominent Zen temple in Japan. The Daitokuji temple in Kyoto, site of the famous sand and rock gardens so much a symbol of Zen all over the world, and home to priceless art objects such as Muji's unequaled Six Persimmons, *is still an important center of Zen. It has produced prominent Zen disciples for centuries.*

Born into a samurai family, Daito began his Buddhist studies at the age of ten. He reached his enlightenment under the tutelage of a master named Daio. When his master died, he left behind a certificate sanctioning Daito as his successor. However, appended to the certificate was the stipulation that Daito spend twenty years in solitary spiritual practice before making his status public.

According to legend, Daito spent much of this time living with beggars beneath a bridge. The emperor, himself a student of Zen, went in disguise to find this man, rumored to be a Zen master. He knew only that the object of his search had a fondness for a certain melon.

The emperor went to the bridge and offered each beggar an armful of melons. As each man came up to him, the emperor examined him carefully. Upon finding one with unusually bright eyes, the emperor held out the melon and said, "Take this without using your hands." When the beggar immediately responded, "Offer it without using your hands," the emperor knew that he had found Daito.

AUTUMN MISO SOUP WITH SWEET POTATO˅

The pale yellow of the sweet potato resembles the full moon of autumn.

Serves 4

5 tablespoons white Kyoto miso
1 tablespoon red miso
3 cups Basic Dashi or Shiitake Dashi (see page 33)
1 small yellow- or orange-fleshed sweet potato
2 teaspoon yellow mustard powder (English, Chinese, or Japanese)

Place the miso in a Japanese mortar (suribachi), or a blender or food processor, and grind until smooth. Continue grinding while gradually adding the dashi. Pass the miso soup through a fine-mesh sieve. Discard the miso solids from the sieve and strain the soup two more times.

Wash the sweet potato; do not peel it. Slice into 1/2-inch rounds with beveled edges. Simmer the rounds in lightly salted water until barely cooked.

Dissolve the mustard powder in enough hot water to form a thick paste. Cover and let sit for at least 10 minutes to deepen the flavor. Thin the mustard paste with 2 tablespoons of the miso soup.

To serve, bring the miso soup to a simmer. Do not let it boil. Place the sweet potato rounds in four covered lacquered soup bowls. Carefully ladle in the hot miso soup. The soup should not cover the sweet potato. Place a drop of mustard on the sweet potato, cover the bowl with the lid, and serve.

CRAB WITH WHITE RADISH SPROUTS

Sprouts of the daikon radish add a peppery note to this saladlike dish. If daikon sprouts are not available, watercress or arugula can be substituted. Please note that the dressing must be made the night before you prepare this dish so that the flavors can develop.

Serves 4

4 ounces daikon radish sprouts
5 1/2 ounces cooked white crab meat

FOR THE DRESSING
1/2 cup soy sauce
1 tablespoon sake
2 teaspoons mirin (*sweet rice wine*)
1 piece konbu (*dried kelp*), 2 inches square
4 tablespoons hana katsuo (*dried bonito flakes*)

Mix together the dressing ingredients. Cover and let stand overnight at room temperature. Strain before using.

Rinse the daikon sprouts and remove the root end. Cut the sprouts in half. If you are using watercress or arugula, rinse and cut into bite-sized pieces.

Pour the dressing into four individual serving dishes.

Toss the crab and sprouts together and lightly pile on top of the dressing. Serve immediately.

TATSUTA TOFU, CHANTERELLES, SPINACH, AND LEMON PEEL^v

The Tatsuta river near Nara has long been celebrated in poetry for its magnificent autumn foliage. The image of the transparent waters of the Tatsuta river dappled with crimson and scarlet autumn leaves is often found on ceramics used for autumn chanoyu gatherings. The colors and flavors of this dish are redolent with the images of autumn.

To prepare this dish you will need two bamboo sushi rolling mats, each approximately 9 inches square, cheesecloth or muslin, and kitchen string.

Serves 4

FOR THE TATSUTA TOFU
14-ounce block firm tofu
3 tablespoons carrot diced into 1/8-inch pieces
2 tablespoons green beans diced into 1/8-inch pieces
1 tablespoon flour
1 tablespoon sugar
1/2 teaspoon salt
1 teaspoon sake
2 tablespoons yellow bell pepper diced into 1/8-inch pieces.

THE OTHER INGREDIENTS
3 cups Basic Dashi or Shiitake Dashi *(see page 33)*, seasoned with sake, soy sauce, and salt to taste
4 large chanterelles *(other fresh wild mushrooms may be substituted)*, cleaned and each cut in half
12 large spinach leaves, parboiled until wilted
4 strips lemon peel, each 2 inches long and 1/8 inch wide

Rinse the tofu in cold water. Drain by placing it on a cutting board, covering it with a plate, and weighting with a large can of food. Let drain for 1 hour.

Parboil the carrot and green beans. Dry them on paper towels. Place the tofu in a bowl and mash with a fork. Do not make the tofu too smooth. Blend in the flour, sugar, salt, and sake. Add the vegetables.

Place a dampened double layer of cheesecloth on the rolling mats. Place half of the tofu mixture in a 1 x 2-inch bar along the length of each mat. Roll up the mats into tight logs. Secure with string.

Place the tofu rolls in a preheated steamer over medium-high heat for 15 minutes.

Remove the tofu rolls and allow them to cool. Remove the mats and cheesecloth. Trim off the ends of each roll to make them even. Cut the rolls into quarters.

Heat the dashi to just below a boil. Add the chanterelles and allow to cook for a moment. The mushrooms will shrink considerably, but their flavor will add depth to the broth.

Place two pieces of the tofu in each bowl. Carefully arrange two chanterelle halves to the left front of the tofu. Place three leaves of spinach to the right front of the tofu. Ladle in 3/4 cup of the seasoned dashi. Top the arrangement with the lemon peel, cover the bowls, and serve.

BAKED TROUT WITH SEA URCHIN GLAZE

Sea urchins have a sweet, nutty flavor. Even in Japan, fresh sea urchins are something of a luxury. Those not destined for the sushi bar usually end up seasoned and bottled for uses such as this glaze. Sea urchin paste, called neri uni in Japanese, is sold in small bottles and is available in most Japanese markets. If you cannot find sea urchin paste, a simple glaze of the sake mixed with 1 egg yolk is also delicious.

Other firm, mild fish can be substituted for the trout.

Serves 4

1 trout, about 1 pound
Salt
3 tablespoons sea urchin paste
1 1/2 teaspoons sake

Preheat oven to 350°F. Skin and fillet the trout. Rinse the fillets in cold water and dry on paper towels. Lightly sprinkle each fillet with salt and let sit for 5 minutes. Rinse and dry the fillets again, and cut each in half.

Lightly oil a baking pan large enough to hold the fillets in a single layer. Arrange the fillets in the pan.

In a small bowl, blend the sea urchin paste and sake to make a glaze. Brush the fillets with the sea urchin glaze.

Bake in the oven for 5 minutes. Brush with more sea urchin glaze and bake for 5 more minutes or until the fish is firm and cooked through.

Remove the fillets to a warmed dish and serve.

MUSCAT GRAPES WITH
YELLOW CHRYSANTHEMUM PETALS^v

Vine-ripened grapes are one of the bounties of autumn. For this recipe, Muscat grapes are served with lightly-vinegared yellow chrysanthemum petals, which have a slightly bitter taste and are often used to garnish autumn foods. Make certain to use organic flowers.

Serves 4

20 large Muscat grapes
2 organically grown yellow
chrysanthemum blossoms
1 tablespoon + 1/2 cup rice vinegar
2 teaspoons sugar

Wash and peel the grapes. Using a toothpick, remove the seeds.

Wash the chrysanthemums and pluck off and save the outer petals. The small inner petals tend to be bitter, so do not use them.

Place the large chrysanthemum petals in a bowl of cold water and rinse. Take care not to bruise them. Drain.

Bring a medium saucepan of water to a boil. Add the 1 tablespoon of rice vinegar. Using a strainer, quickly plunge the chrysanthemum petals into the boiling water and then drain immediately. Place the parboiled petals into a bowl of cold water. When the petals are cool, drain them and gently press out the excess water.

Place the remaining rice vinegar and the sugar in a glass or other nonreactive bowl. Stir until the sugar has dissolved. Add the chrysanthemum petals and grapes to the sweetened vinegar and toss.

Place in a bowl and serve.

LIGHT BROTH FLAVORED WITH WALNUTS ^v

The rich flavor of new-crop walnuts is featured in this dish.

Serves 4

2 new-crop walnuts
1 cup water
1 piece konbu (*dried kelp*), approximately
2 x 5 inches

Shell the walnuts. Place half a walnut in each serving cup.

Bring the water to a boil. Add the dried kelp and remove from the heat. Leave the kelp in the hot water for 1 minute, then remove. The flavor should be very subtle.

Pour 4 tablespoons of the flavored hot water into each cup, cover, and serve.

CHESTNUT BALLS AND GRILLED PEPPERS ^v

Chestnut purée, formed into balls, is paired with the smoky, sweet taste of roasted red bell peppers. If you are serving this on a cedar hassun tray, place the chestnut balls on the upper right-hand side and the red pepper strips on the lower left-hand side. If you are not serving this dish in the kaiseki manner, you can expand the recipe.

Serves 4

12 large chestnuts
Sake
Sugar
Salt to taste
1 medium red bell pepper

Rinse the chestnuts and cut each in half using a cleaver or heavy chef's knife. Place them in a pan and cover with cold water. Bring to a boil, then reduce the heat and simmer for 5 to 10 minutes. The chestnuts are done when you can pierce the meat easily with a toothpick.

Drain the chestnuts. Using a small spoon, carefully scoop the chestnut meat from the shell and place it in a Japanese mortar (suribachi) or bowl. Chestnuts are covered with a brown papery skin that tastes rather bitter. Usually, if you remove the chestnuts from the shell while they are still hot, the skin will remain in the shell. If some skin adheres to the chestnut meat, carefully pick it off.

Using a pestle or wooden spoon, crush the chestnut meats into a medium-fine paste. Leave a few larger pieces to lend contrast. The consistency should resemble lumpy mashed potatoes. Thin the chestnut paste with some sake. The exact amount varies according to your taste and the consistency of the chestnut paste. Do not make it too thin. Add a pinch each of sugar and salt. Divide the chestnut paste into six equal portions. Roll each portion into a ball about the size of a large marble. Place the chestnut balls in an airtight container until ready to serve.

Grill the red pepper. The most efficient way to do this is to place the pepper directly on a gas burner, turning it as the skin begins to char. If you do not have a gas stove, grill the pepper under the broiler. Once the pepper skin has charred all over, place it in a small paper bag and let sit for about 15 minutes. Remove the pepper from the bag. The charred skin should peel off quite easily. Remove the stem and seeds from the pepper and cut into six even strips.

Place the chestnut balls in the upper right and the red pepper strips in the lower left of a tray and serve.

GREEN TOMATO-MISO PICKLES, VINEGARED CUCUMBER, AND TAKUAN WITH BROWNED RICE-CRUST SOUP^v

Pickled in white miso, the green tomatoes of autumn make a deliciously tart addition to this course, together with vinegared cucumber and takuan. Be sure to start this recipe the day before you plan to serve it. Following the same method, you can reuse the miso in this recipe to pickle other vegetables such as celery, eggplant, and zucchini.

Serves 4

8 pieces takuan
Vinegared Cucumbers *(see page 132)*

FOR THE GREEN TOMATO-MISO PICKLES
1 large green *(slightly underripe)* **tomato**
Salt
3 cups white or beige miso paste

To prepare the green tomato pickles, rinse and quarter the tomato. Lightly salt the tomato quarters and let sit for 10 minutes. Pat dry with paper towels. Place the miso paste in a glass or other nonreactive dish. Submerge the tomato quarters in the miso and let sit overnight.

Remove the tomato quarters. Rinse each quarter and cut into 1/8-inch slices.

Rinse the takuan and cut into pieces 1/4-inch thick. Trim these pieces into rectangular shapes.

Arrange all the pickles in separate heaps on a plate. Serve with Browned Rice-Crust Soup (see page 126).

A WINTER KAISEKI MENU

First Course
Rice
Miso Soup with Lotus Root
Smoked Sturgeon with Belgian Endive and Capers

Second Course
Shrimp and Fresh Shiitake Mushrooms with Grated Radish

Third Course
Seared Sake-Marinated Scallops

Fourth Course
Simmered Winter Squash

Fifth Course
Light Broth Flavored with Cranberries

Sixth Course
Poached Oysters with Preserved Lemon Peel

Seventh Course
Lightly Salted White Radish
Takuan
Browned Rice-Crust Soup

Eighth Course
Tea Sweets or Pears

MISO SOUP WITH LOTUS ROOT ᵛ

This winter miso soup relies on the rich, sweet taste of Kyoto white miso. Lotus root cut into rounds resembles snowflakes, giving this soup the appearance of snow piled in a silver bowl.

Lotus roots grow in a series of pod shapes. The shorter, rounder sections are more tender than the long and thick ones (these are best used in stews or soups cooked for a long time). If possible, use fresh lotus roots, selecting pieces with unblemished skin and no dark spots. Vacuum-packed lotus roots are now available as well.

Serves 4

6 tablespoons white Kyoto miso
3 cups Basic Dashi or Shiitake Dashi (see page 33)
1 small lotus root, enough to yield two or three ¼-inch
rounds per serving
Rice vinegar
2 teaspoons yellow mustard powder (English, Chinese, or Japanese)

Place the miso in a Japanese mortar (suribachi), or a blender or food processor, and grind until smooth. While grinding, gradually add the dashi. Pass the miso through a fine-mesh sieve. Discard the miso solids from the sieve and strain the miso soup two more times. The miso soup can be set aside for several hours at room temperature, and then heated just before serving.

Wash the lotus root. Using a vegetable peeler, peel off the tan skin. Slice the lotus root into ¼-inch rounds and bevel the cut edges. You could also trim off the outer circumference of the lotus root slices to produce a more realistic snowflake shape. Immediately drop the slices into a bowl of cold water to which you have added 1 teaspoon rice vinegar. (This will keep the lotus root from discoloring.)

Drain the lotus root just before parboiling.

Fill a medium saucepan with cold water and add 1 teaspoon rice vinegar and a pinch of salt. Bring the water to a boil. Parboil the lotus root rounds for about 3 to 5 minutes or until just cooked.

Dissolve the mustard powder in enough hot water to form a thick paste. Cover and let sit for at least 10 minutes to deepen the flavor. Thin the mustard paste with 2 tablespoons of the miso soup.

Bring the miso soup to a simmer. Do not let it boil as this will make it taste very harsh. Place two or three rounds of lotus root in each covered lacquered soup bowl. Carefully ladle in the hot miso soup. The soup should not cover the lotus root. Place a drop of mustard on the lotus root, cover the bowls with the lids, and serve.

SMOKED STURGEON WITH BELGIAN ENDIVE AND CAPERS

This simple and easily prepared combination of Western ingredients lends itself well to a kaiseki meal. The bittersweet endive and salty capers are a perfect foil for the rich taste of smoked sturgeon.

Serves 4

12 thin slices smoked sturgeon
1 small Belgian endive
1 tablespoon fresh lemon juice
1 tablespoon capers

Cut each slice of smoked sturgeon in half. Roll up the smoked sturgeon slices and lightly stack six rolls on each individual serving dish.

Rinse the endive and remove the root end. Slice the endive crosswise into thin strips. Toss the endive strips with the lemon juice.

Garnish the salmon rolls with the endive. Sprinkle the capers on top of the sturgeon. Serve immediately.

SHRIMP AND FRESH SHIITAKE MUSHROOMS WITH GRATED RADISH

There are many recipes for kabura mushi, the Japanese name for this savory winter dish. Regardless of the variations, they all rely upon the gently warming taste of daikon, the white radish also called mooli. If you cannot find daikon, try substituting an equivalent amount of grated baby turnips. The taste will be slightly different, but just as delicious.

Serves 4

9 raw medium shrimp or prawns, peeled and deveined
9 medium fresh shiitake mushrooms
9 sprigs (stems and leaves) of Japanese parsley *(mitsuba)* or flat-leaf parsley
1 medium daikon radish, about 10 inches long
Salt
2 egg whites
3 cups Basic Dashi or Shiitake Dashi *(see page 33)*, seasoned to taste with sake and soy sauce
2 teaspoons arrowroot or cornstarch
2 teaspoons finely grated fresh ginger

Cut the shrimp in half lengthwise.

Remove the stems from the mushrooms and cut the caps into quarters.

Blanch the parsley. Cut stems so whole leaves form bite-sized pieces.

Toss together the shrimp, shiitake mushrooms, and parsley. Divide this mixture among four small, shallow heatproof dishes.

Preheat a large steamer.

Trim the top and root end of the daikon. (reserve these for use in the winter pickle recipe). Thickly peel the daikon, then finely grate until you have 1 cup. Any remaining daikon can be reserved for another use, or used in the winter pickle recipe. Pour the grated daikon (it will be watery) into a fine sieve and lightly press out most of the liquid. Transfer the pressed grated daikon to a bowl and sprinkle with a pinch of salt.

Whisk the egg whites until they are light and foamy, but still moist. Do not overwhisk. Combine the grated daikon and the egg whites. Gently dome the daikon mixture over the shrimp mixture. Steam for about 10 to 12 minutes at medium-high heat.

Bring the seasoned dashi to a simmer. Mix the arrowroot or cornstarch with a small amount of cold dashi or water and add to the simmering dashi, stirring until the dashi becomes slightly thick.

Carefully place one daikon dome in each lidded serving bowl. Ladle the thickened dashi to the side of the bowl, not on top of the domes. Place 1/2 teaspoon freshly grated ginger on top of the daikon domes. Cover the bowls and serve immediately.

SEARED SAKE-MARINATED SCALLOPS

This is a very simple yet delicious recipe *(see opposite)*. Two large scallops per person is sufficient if you are serving this dish as part of the winter kaiseki menu. The secret to this recipe is to cook the scallops very briefly over a high heat.

Serves 4

½ cup sake
Soy sauce to taste
8 large scallops
Salt to taste
1 teaspoon vegetable oil

Season the sake lightly with soy sauce. Marinate the scallops in the seasoned sake for 20 minutes. Remove the scallops from the marinade and drain on paper towels. Lightly salt the scallops.

Lightly oil a nonstick sauté pan and place over high heat. Sear the scallops for 2 to 3 minutes on each side. The scallops should be slightly firm to the touch. Place the scallops on a preheated serving dish and serve immediately.

SIMMERED WINTER SQUASH ᵛ

The Japanese winter squash, kabocha, has a dense texture and sweet, nutty flavor. It ripens in the warm sun of late summer. Kabocha squash stores very well and is usually served as a part of autumn and winter meals in Japan. It is one of the foods eaten during the cold winter months to ensure good health. Acorn or any other dense-fleshed winter squash can be prepared in this way.

Serves 4

1 small kabocha squash

FOR THE SIMMERING LIQUID
1 cup Basic Dashi or Shiitake Dashi *(see page 33)*
1½ cups water
4 tablespoons sugar
3 tablespoons sake
1 teaspoon salt

Cut the squash in half and scoop out the seeds and fibers. Slice the squash into wedges about 2 inches thick. Using a vegetable peeler, remove most of the skin from the squash wedges.

In a saucepan large enough to hold the squash in a single layer, combine the ingredients for the simmering liquid and stir until the sugar is dissolved. Add the squash wedges and bring to a gentle simmer. Gently simmer the squash for 15 to 20 minutes or until done. Remove the cooked squash to a plate, reserving the simmering liquid.

Place the squash wedges in a warmed bowl and pour some of the simmering liquid over them. Any leftover squash can be stored in an airtight container and eaten the next day.

LIGHT BROTH FLAVORED WITH CRANBERRIES˅

While cranberries are not a traditional ingredient of kaiseki cooking, their sweet-tart taste lends itself well to this dish.

Serves 4

4 small cranberries, washed
1 cup water
1 piece konbu *(dried kelp),* approximately
2 x 5 inches

Place one cranberry in each serving cup.

Bring the water to a boil. Add the dried kelp and remove from the heat. Leave the kelp in the hot water for 1 minute, then remove. The flavor should be very subtle.

Pour 4 tablespoons of the flavored hot water into each cup, cover, and serve.

POACHED OYSTERS WITH PRESERVED LEMON PEEL

For the winter kaiseki menu, the elemental flavor of poached oysters is balanced by the bright, sweet taste of the preserved lemon peel. The standard amount of food for the hassun course allows for one piece of each food for each guest and the host, plus one serving to be left on the tray.

The proportions listed below are for a kaiseki meal for four guests. You may increase the proportions of these recipes to suit the occasion. The preserved lemon should be prepared the day before. The oysters should be prepared no more than a few hours in advance of serving.

Serves 4

6 small freshly shucked oysters

FOR THE PRESERVED LEMON PEEL
1 Meyer or other lemon
1½ cups sugar
1 cup water

FOR THE POACHING LIQUID
1 cup Basic Dashi or Shiitake Dashi
(see page 33)
4 tablespoons sake
2 tablespoons soy sauce
A pinch of salt

To prepare the preserved lemon, wash the lemon well and cut into quarters. Using a very sharp knife, remove the lemon pulp, including the white pith next to the colored part of the lemon peel. Discard the lemon pulp and pith. Place the quarters of lemon peel in a bowl of cold water and soak for 1 hour.

Bring a medium saucepan of water to a boil. Add the lemon peel and boil for 1 minute. Drain the lemon peel. Repeat this procedure two more times.

Combine the sugar and water in a small saucepan. Over medium heat, stir until the sugar has dissolved, then bring the mixture to a simmer. Add the lemon peel. Cook the lemon peel at a low simmer until it is easily pierced with a toothpick, about 8 to 10 minutes. Remove from the heat and let cool.

Place the lemon peel and sugar syrup in a bowl, cover, and let sit overnight.

Combine the ingredients for the poaching liquid in a small saucepan and bring to a gentle simmer. Add the oysters and poach for 2 to 3 minutes or until the edges of the oysters begin to curl. Remove the oysters to a bowl and let cool. Strain the poaching liquid and allow to cool. Pour the strained poaching liquid over the oysters and refrigerate.

Remove the lemon peel from the sugar syrup and drain on paper towels. Cut each piece in half. Drain the poached oysters.

Lightly dampen a cedar hassun tray. Place the lemon peel on the upper right corner and the oysters in the lower left corner of the hassun tray. Serve immediately.

LIGHTLY SALTED WHITE RADISH AND TAKUAN WITH BROWNED RICE-CRUST SOUP ^v

The frugal nature of this recipe is in keeping with the spirit of Zen and kaiseki cooking. The peelings and any leftover pieces of daikon radish, along with whatever leafy greens that are attached, are cut into matchsticks, lightly salted, and flavored with dried chiles and dried kelp. You can serve white radish pickles with takuan or any of the other pickles listed in the kaiseki recipes as part of this course.

The white radish pickles should be prepared at least the day before you serve them. They will keep, refrigerated, for up to 2 days.

Serves 4

8 pieces takuan

FOR THE SALTED WHITE RADISH
1 pound daikon radish, including peelings of skin and green leaves
1 1/2 tablespoons salt (seasalt is best)
2 pieces konbu (dried kelp), each about 1 1/4 x 5 inches
2 or 3 dried Japanese red peppers (or any other small dried hot red chile)

To prepare the salted white radish, cut the daikon into matchstick-sized pieces. Toss with the salt and place in a nonreactive strainer over a large bowl. Let drain for 2 hours. The daikon will become limp and exude a slightly greenish liquid. Discard the liquid.

Place one piece of dried kelp on the bottom of a shallow rectangular glass dish. Place the salted daikon on top of the dried kelp. Place the dried chiles on top of the salted daikon, sprinkle lightly with salt, and cover with the other piece of dried kelp. Cover the pickles with wax paper or plastic wrap. Press the pickles by placing another glass container, lid, plate, or weight on top. Let the pickles mature overnight or up to 2 days in the refrigerator. Remove the dried kelp and red peppers before serving.

Rinse the takuan and cut into pieces 1/4 inch thick. Trim these pieces into rectangular shapes.

Arrange both of the pickles in separate heaps on a plate. Serve with Browned Rice-Crust Soup (see page 126).

TABLE OF NAMES

Zen is the Japanese translation of the Chinese name Chan (Ch'an). Chan, a sect of Buddhism, originated in India, and developed in China under the influence of Taoism. During the thirteenth century, it evolved still further in Japan under the name Zen.

The majority of classic Zen writings come from either Chinese or Japanese sources. In the process of many translations, a particular term may be known differently in various languages but have the same meaning. For example, the term Zen is identical with the original Sanskrit name dhyana, but unless one knows that, it is possible to go for years thinking the two terms are different. Further confusion results if a reader is unaware that some names have simply been transliterated differently. For example, the name of Zen master, Baizhang Huaihai, is also written as Pai-Chang Huai-Hai, or Hyakujo Yekai.

In this book, words have been spelled according to their native reference. If a word or master's name was originally Chinese, the native version of that name has been spelled using the pinyin system. However, since many Zen texts still utilize the Wade-Giles system of Romanization, the table at right gives the equivalent spelling. If the name plays such an important role in Japanese Zen that it has taken on a Japanese equivalent, that term also appears in the table. If a term is purely Japanese, such as the case of the name of a Japanese Zen master or a Japanese word, that term appears solely in Japanese Romanization. In the same way, Bodhidharma, who was from India, is spelled in the Indian way.

Technically, we should refer to Chan when referring to Chinese tradition and Zen when referring to the Japanese. However, for simplicity's sake, only the word Zen has been used. The interested reader is invited to explore the rich world of Zen, and to trace its fascinating evolution from India through China, into Japan, and eventually throughout the world.

A few words have taken on an independent identity in the English language—such as the word Tao. Those terms that appear in English dictionaries have been left in their most recognizable form, regardless of the system of Romanization.

The chief language is indicated in bold. The other column shows spellings from India (I) or other older spellings (O) that may not be tied to any system of Romanization, but may still be recognized.

PINYIN	WADE-GILES	JAPANESE	OTHER
Baizhang	Huaihai	Pai-Chang Huai-Hai	Hyakujo Yekai
Chan	Ch'an	**Zen**	dhyana (I)
Dao De Jing	Tao Te Ching		
Dao	Tao	Do	
fangshi	fang shih		
Gongchun	Kung Ch'un		
gongfu	kung fu		
Han Zhongli	Han Chung-Li		
Hanshan Deqing		Han-Shan Te-Ching	
Huineng	Hui-Neng	Eno	
jing	ching		
Kung Fuzi	K'ung Fu-Tzu	Confucius (O)	
Lao Zi	Lao-Tzu		
Li Xizhen	Li Shih-Chen		
lingzi	ling tzu	rishi	
Linji Yixuan	Lin-Chi I-Hsuan	Rinzai Gigen	
Liu An	Liu An		
Longjing	Lung Ching		
Lu Dongbin	Lu Tung-Pin		
Lu Yu	Lu Yu		
luohan	lohan		
Mazu Daoyi	Ma-tzu Tao-i	Baso Doichi	
Meng Zi	Meng-Tzu	Moshi	Mencius (O)
Muji	Mu-Ch'i	Mokkei	
Nanchuan Puyuan	Nan-ch'uan P'u-yuan	Nansen Fugwan	
Pen Cao	P'en Ts'ao		
Pu Er	P'u Erh		
Puti Damo	P'u-t'i Ta-Mo	Bodai Daruma	**Bodhidharma** (I)
qi	ch'i	ki	prana (I)
Qin Shihuang	Ch'in Shih-Huang		
Qing (dynasty)	Ch'ing		
Shen Nong	Shen Nung		
shen	shen		
Song (dynasty)	Sung		
Tang (dynasty)	T'ang		
Tieguanyin	T'ieh Kuan-Yin		
Wu Yishan	Wu I-Shan		
Wulong	Wu Lung		Oolong (O)
Xiangpian	Hsiang P'ien		
Yi Jing	*I Ching*		
Yixing	I Hsing		
zhai	chai		
Zhou (dynasty)	Chou		
Zhuang Zi	Chuang-tzu		

BIBLIOGRAPHY

Brown, Edward Espe. *Tomato Blessings and Radish Teachings.* New York: Riverhead, 1997

Chang, Kwang-chih, (ed.) *Food in Chinese Culture.* New Haven: Yale, 1997

Chow, Kit, I. Kramer. *All the Tea in China.* San Francisco: China Books, 1990

Foster, N. J. Shoemaker, eds. *The Roaring Stream.* Hopewell: Ecco, 1996

Koren, Leonard. *Wabi-Sabi for Artists, Designers, Poets, and Philosophers.* Berkeley: Stone Bridge Press, 1994

Okakura, Kakuzo. *The Book of Tea.* Tokyo: Kodansha, 1989

Reps, Paul. *Zen Flesh, Zen Bones.* Rutland: Charles E. Tuttle, 1983

Saso, Michael. *A Taoist Cookbook.* Rutland: Charles E. Tuttle, 1994

Sen, Soshitsu. *Tea Life, Tea Mind.* New York: Weatherhill, 1979

— *Chado.* New York: Weatherhill, 1979

Suzuki, D. T. *Zen Buddhism and Japanese Culture.* New York: Princeton, 1959

Suzuki, Shunryu. *Zen Mind, Beginner's Mind.* New York: Weatherhill, 1970

Tani, Kogetsu. *Zen Word, Zen Calligraphy.* Boston: Shambhala, 1990

Tonkinson, Carole, (ed.) *Wake Up and Cook.* New York: Riverhead, 1997

Tsuji, Kaichi. *Kaiseki.* Tokyo: Kodansha, 1972

Uchiyama, Kosho. *From the Zen Kitchen to Enlightenment.* New York: Weatherhill, 1994

Vitell, Betina. *The World in a Bowl of Tea.* New York: HarperCollins, 1997

Wong, Eva. *The Shambhala Guide to Taoism.* Boston: Shambhala, 1997

Wu, Ching-Hsiung. *The Golden Age of Zen.* New York: Image, 1996

Yanagi, Soetsu. *The Unknown Craftsman.* Tokyo: Kadansha, 1972

Yoneda, Soei. *The Heart of Zen Cuisine.* Tokyo: Kodansha, 1982

Zee, A. *Swallowing Clouds,* New York: Simon & Schuster, 1990

INDEX